Teen CRaft Projects 2

Teen Craft Projects 2

Tina Coleman and Peggie Llanes

Foreword by Amy Alessio and Katie LaMantia

ala
editions

An imprint of the American Library Association
Chicago | 2013

Tina Coleman is membership specialist for the membership development department of the American Library Association, as well as staff liaison to both the Virtual Communities in Libraries Member Interest Group and the Comics and Graphic Novels in Libraries Member Interest Group. Often recognized as ALA's "on-staff fan-girl," she also writes fiction and poetry, reviews books for *Booklist* magazine, and is an avid music aficionado. She's a crafter and artist who works on projects on her own and with her mother for sale locally. Her work at ALA has given her an insider's view of the library world and a way to apply her multiple creative talents.

Peggie Llanes worked for many years at Christopher House, a Chicago day care and social services center, where she had extensive training in child development, social service, and community and group work. Through her experience working with underprivileged children, she developed a keen sense of the importance of presenting open-ended projects that promote creativity and individuality and enhance self-esteem. Beyond crafting and developing new projects, she is also currently an active volunteer and board member of St. Mary of Providence, a residential facility for adult women with developmental disabilities. Her biggest joy over the past year has been seeing how going through many of these craft projects has helped her daughter, Melissa, who has developmental delays, increase her skill levels, concentration, and self-expression.

Printed in the United States of America
17 16 15 14 13   5 4 3 2 1

Extensive effort has gone into ensuring the reliability of the information in this book; however, the publisher makes no warranty, express or implied, with respect to the material contained herein.

ISBNs: 978-0-8389-1152-5 (paper); 978-0-8389-9659-1 (PDF). For more information on digital formats, visit the ALA Store at alastore.ala.org and select eEditions.

Library of Congress Cataloging-in-Publication Data

Coleman, Tina.
    Teen craft projects 2 / Tina Coleman and Peggie Llanes ; foreword by Amy Alessio and Katie LaMantia.
        pages   cm
    Includes index.
    ISBN 978-0-8389-1152-5 (alk. paper)
    1. Young adults' libraries—Activity programs. 2. Libraries and teenagers.
3. Handicraft. I. Llanes, Peggie. II. Title. III. Title: Teen craft projects two.
Z718.5.C625 2013
027.62'6—dc23
                                                                    2012041728

Book design by Kimberly Thornton in Charis SIL and ITC American Typewriter.

♾ This paper meets the requirements of ANSI/NISO Z39.48-1992 (Permanence of Paper).

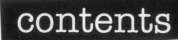

contents

**S TEENS LOOK FOR WAYS TO EXPRESS THEMSELVES,** they often turn to crafts. Crafting fulfills several important developmental needs for this age group. In addition to helping young adults explore their creativity and learn new skills, it opens the way for them to socialize and build confidence. Teen crafters can link up with like-minded others and become part of a group, and success with a project can lead them to a hobby or art form they'll enjoy the rest of their lives. The library offers a great setting for teen crafts, but dealing with shrinking staff and resource budgets is a continuing challenge, as is finding crafts simple enough for the inexperienced yet challenging enough to give talented crafters room to grow.

Teens and staff at the Schaumburg Township District Library were thrilled to be asked to test the crafts for this special resource. Kids in grades 6 through high school participated. All found something to like, and the projects inspired some staff to learn new skills. Librarian-student Katie LaMantia, herself a graduate of the library's teen services programs, worked with author Tina Coleman to coordinate the projects. A few of the crafts were tested by a small group of girls in evening programs; more often, they were tested by our entire Teen Corps group, of which about half are boys. The crafts had the teens clamoring to participate, something Tina experienced firsthand when she attended a Teen Corps meeting where a craft was being tested. The teens descended upon the supplies and instructions in a flurry of controlled chaos. There is now interest in a crafting club at the library.

Katie found the experience of working with teens and Tina to be invaluable. One of her favorite crafts was creating memory boards. Although it's a very simple craft, it offered lots of opportunities for kids to express themselves using different fabrics, ribbons, beads and buttons, and other materials. Teens could be as minimalist or as accessory-crazy as they wanted. It was great for the librarians, too, because it required minimal setup and no special tools. Participants didn't always proceed exactly as the instructions were written, but these projects have been developed in such a way that crafters could easily make them their own. Discovering they wanted to make wall hangings instead of no-sew organizers, a few boys bonded and surprised the staff with some exceptionally inventive neon collages. Boys enjoyed many of the crafts, tailoring each with a unique touch. One of Katie's favorite reactions came from a normally hyperactive eighth-grade boy who was creating a no-sew organizer: "Wow. This is actually fun!" Coming from a teenage boy, this is the highest praise.

Katie sent Tina summaries of the teens' reactions to the projects, along with photos and tips for making the book as practical as possible for libraries of all sizes. Staff agreed that participating in the testing gave Schaumburg Township teens the chance to let loose their inner artist. All the tweens and teens enjoyed being part of the creative process and experimenting with the various media and supplies. They also appreciated that their ideas and opinions were being used to help improve the crafting instructions.

Allowing for a variety of skill levels and activities, this book is a great resource for developing popular, cost-effective, ecologically responsible teen craft programs that are really fun.

—*Amy Alessio and Katie LaMantia*

acknowledgments

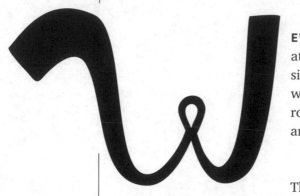

WE'D LIKE TO TAKE A MOMENT TO THANK THE FOLKS at Schaumburg Township District Library: Amy Alessio and Katie LaMantia and all of the kids in their wonderful Teen Corps group. They took our work and road tested the projects to make sure they worked and were loads of fun.

Thanks to Tina for inviting me back for a second round of crafting and writing and for encouraging me to stretch my creativity. She always reminds me that one is never too old to learn something new and that I may know a trick or two that I can share with others. I hope we will continue to inspire each other to always be open to new discoveries.

Thanks also to my hubby, Ray, for his support and encouragement and for not complaining about a messy house and many days and nights of crafting. He is still our biggest fan!

Thanks to my daughter, Melissa, for trying to help us with our projects and for always keeping a keen eye out for recycled supplies. Also thanks to the rest of my family and friends who continue to support our endeavors. It is clear to me that they are really listening to the recycle, repurpose ideas behind our crafting projects because they always bring us more materials to work with and challenge us to come up with new projects for them.

—*Peggie Llanes*

There are so many people that helped us write this book. Many thanks to the ALA Editions crew, especially Stephanie for advising and giving us a hard deadline when we really needed it. Thanks to John for being not only an awesome boss, but a good sounding board as well. Thanks to Pat for templates and tutorials and tons of ideas. Thanks to Dad for food and his truckload of enthusiasm for every project. Thanks to Jérôme, who managed to be helpful from a thousand miles away, especially in the creation of robots and card games. Thanks to Mel, for being as patient as she's able, and thanks to Sofiana and Megan and all of my wonderfully creative and inspirational friends.

Extra special thanks to the librarians—you are all superheroes.

—*Tina Coleman*

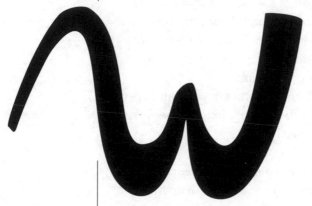

ELCOME TO TEEN CRAFT PROJECTS 2! WHETHER you've dog-eared all the pages in our first book and are desperate for more, or you're just beginning your crafting endeavors, in this volume you'll find twelve cool craft projects to do with your teen group. From turning that stack of old magazines and catalogs into stationery to baking your own army of adorable clay creatures, we've got some doozies covered.

In developing this batch of projects, we consciously set out to come up with ideas that would engage teens of all stripes—boys, girls, geeks, hipsters, artists, activists, fans, and even a few smarty-pants types. We're pleased to present a dozen opportunities for your teens to get creative making their own flashy flair, their own decor, and even their own games. We encourage not only the teens, but also you, the librarian, to exercise your imagination and let your unique style shine through.

One of the new aspects of this book is the addition of a quick-fire version for most of the projects. With sports, clubs, SAT prep, after-school jobs, homework, band practice, and a host of other activities competing for their attention, teens can often be pressed for time. We know that while you may want to present some programming, your teens may not have two or three hours to do a full-length project. Thus, we try to give you some tips on how to accomplish each project in a simple 40-minute program. Two main time-savers are to take on more of the prep work yourself and to limit the creative choices. We recommend doing the full version of the project whenever possible.

Along with the quick-fire versions, we've also included some hints on how you might think about a craft differently in order to adapt it to other groups or programs: from providing more sophisticated materials for adults and seniors, to scaling things down for younger kids, to organizing parent-child or other shared community projects. We encourage you to look at the projects with an eye toward how they would best fit at your library.

We include some vital statistics in the header of each project:

Difficulty: This will give you an idea of how hard you can expect a project to be. Keep in mind that this gauge of difficulty applies to teens in general. Projects may be more or less difficult depending on age, skill level, experience, and interest.

Time: This is a very general approximation of how long the project should take under optimal conditions (not including cleanup or your prep work). Take your own experience with your teens into account when scheduling your program.

Supervision: This is a guide as to how closely you'll need to monitor the group while they work on the project.

Group Size: This is our recommendation for how many participants you should plan for per adult supervisor. We try to take all of the other factors into consideration for this guideline, and we can't stress enough how important it is to pay attention to your group size. If you have a lot of teens who are interested in a program, consider getting more adult volunteers or staff to help supervise, or break the group into more than one session.

Mess Factor: This is a general warning to you about how messy you can expect your space to get. Kids can make a mess under the best of circumstances with a sort of heroic ability, so mainly just be prepared.

In the end these are all just guidelines. You know your regular teens best, so you should be able to read through the instructions and get a sense of any adjustments you'll need to make. See appendix C for a glossary of terms that might be unfamiliar to you.

To ensure that your program goes smoothly and your teens have fun, you'll need to do a certain amount of prep work ahead of time. As group projects, these don't work well if you're not prepared. With this in mind, we've provided "Getting the Project Ready" and "Getting the Room Ready" sections for each craft. It is *highly recommended* that you follow these directions for group projects. In the long run, it will make your life much easier.

Here's an outline of prep work that you'll need to expect to do for each project:

Read the full set of instructions. This will give you a sense of what each step entails and how the craft goes together. Take this opportunity to make notes about changes you may need to make for your particular group of teens.

Make (or have made) a finished sample. It's important to have a sample on hand so teens have something to refer to when making their own, but you can also use the sample (or samples) to advertise and drum up interest in the program. While our first choice would be for you to make a sample yourself, so you have firsthand experience of the instructions and techniques, you can also have another volunteer or a reliable and crafty member of your teen group make a sample.

Sort and prepare your space and materials. Your program will go much more smoothly if you have your materials prepared and laid out when your group gets started. Your space will be much easier to manage if your tables are covered, wastebaskets are handy, and your supplies, tools, and materials are organized. Often we call for the use of trays or containers of some sort for each participant to keep their working materials together. Most of our recommendations for room layout include a main worktable (or tables) and a separate side table for materials and supplies. This cuts down on confusion and disputes and allows for a better flow.

The basics of almost any crafting program are to know your resources well. Resources include supplies, materials, and tools, of course, but they also include yourself and your own knowledge and creativity, and your teens.

As in our previous book, most of our projects rely heavily on recycled materials. This is better for the environment and better for your budget. When sourcing materials, remember to look around your library first. Often your outdated magazines, catalogs, weeded books, damaged DVDs or CDs, and so on can make up a sizable stash. And don't forget to put the word out to other staff and even your patrons if you're looking for a specific type of item. Recycling for programs can be a great way to make your community feel more connected to the library.

Use your budget wisely when purchasing supplies, materials, and tools. Free or inexpensive materials are all around you. What doesn't come in from donations (or participants bringing their own) you can get from flea markets, thrift shops, garage sales, discount and dollar stores, you name it. Finding things on the Internet can save you cash—lots of materials and tools are available online.

When looking for tools, be frugal but canny. Spending $30 on a grommet setter or two may seem like a luxury, but your group will use them over and over again. Spending the same money on something like stickers is less economical, since they can only be used once, and you can do pretty much the same thing (with more creative results) with some choice paper scrap and decoupage. Likewise, sometimes buying a better quality, but slightly more expensive, product will save you money in the long run. Don't skimp on tools that you'll be using more than once, sewing supplies, packing tape (it's worth it to get the thicker variety), or quick-drying multipurpose glue (we like Quick Glue or E-6000 brands). If you can, invest in a few heavy-duty tablecloths or drop cloths that you can use to cover your tables for multiple sessions.

After getting a load of supplies and materials via donation, thrift shopping, and so on, you'll often need to prep those materials by doing a bit of deconstructing. Deconstructing can be a fun (and educational) group project all on its own. Taking apart a pair of jeans, a leather jacket, or a bag will show you a lot about how those things are made. Breaking apart watches, jewelry, or clocks to get at the parts inside can give you an idea of how they work and how you can remake them into something new. You can even set goals for using every scrap from those pieces that you can. (See projects like Rock Star Jewelry or Recycled Mobiles.)

One thing to keep in mind about the materials and supplies we list in our projects is that almost everything is optional. Our lists are designed to include all of the possible creative options, but you don't need to provide every single thing we suggest. Read through the instructions and decide which materials you really need and which components you want to offer.

Remember, too, that you are a valuable resource unto yourself. You know your teens, your library, and your community best, so you should know what's possible. Be flexible in interpreting our instructions if you need to be. As we always say, there's no right way to do crafts. Feel free to be creative about reworking the rules as needed for your group. Depending on your teens, you may also need to work within their parameters. If you have lefties in your group, be sure to stock some left-handed scissors. If you have teens who are squeamish about messes, having plastic gloves or even wet wipes on hand may be a good solution. If someone is uncomfortable with the tools, try to find ways that he can get the needed result (for instance, ripping paper instead of cutting it).

Another key resource is your regular teen group. As you begin your craft program, it's worth sitting down with them to discuss what they want to work on and what kinds of materials they want to work with. Some may want to stick to projects that give them something to wear once they're done. Some may want ways to spruce up their bedrooms or lockers. Some may just know they want to work with hardware or clay. Giving them a voice early in the process will help them be more engaged in the projects. And it takes some of the pressure off of you to come up with all the different materials. If it's feasible, you can even take a few of them shopping for some of the key ingredients like fabrics or hardware.

Crafting programs in your library can be worthwhile to everyone who contributes to the program, from patrons who donate materials to volunteers who help with projects to the teens who do the crafts themselves. With some vision and a bit of glue you can come up with a program that dazzles the community.

Teens can benefit from crafting in so many ways. Crafts can provide opportunities for creativity and self-expression that teens often struggle to communicate. The skills they learn in crafting can be applied to other areas of life and vice versa; problem solving, teamwork, and self-sufficiency are all skills that can be learned and reinforced through crafting. It can be a focus for discussion and ideas, and even a springboard to learning more.

For example, when we first began this book we knew we wanted to do something with games, but through working on the Make Your Own Games project we learned so much about how traditional games are put together and developed and even revisited the rules to some of our favorite classic games. Working through projects like this will show you new avenues for being truly creative and taking your design into other realms entirely.

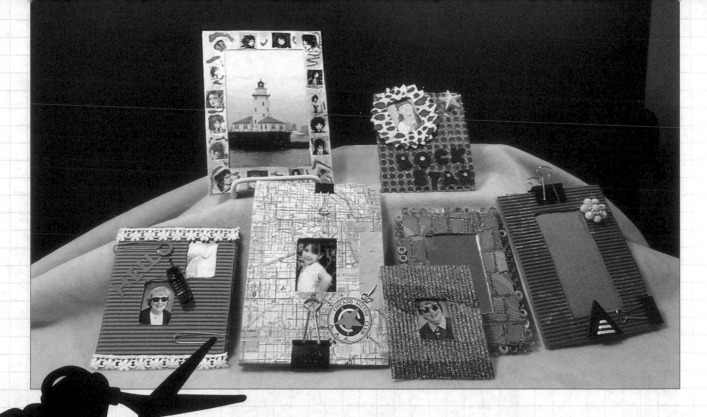

design your own picture frames

Difficulty:
Easy

Time:
60 minutes

Supervision:
Medium

Group Size:
6–8 teens per
librarian

Mess Factor:
Medium

THIS EASY PICTURE FRAME PROJECT CAN BE A FUN DIVER-sion for teens or an opportunity to make gifts for parents, teachers, or friends. The materials can be pulled together and left out for teens to work with as they please. Have photocopies of the instructions ready. As teens come in, hand them the instructions and point them toward your craft table.

Because the focus is really on embellishing the frames, this craft is a good pick for groups or for parent-child crafting programs. Embellishments can be as simple as a light dusting of glitter or as complex as a decoupage design. This flexibility allows teens to be creative whatever their level of craft experience.

The project also gives you the chance to recycle things you have on hand, and it can easily be adapted to suit preexisting programs on recycling or the environment. Cardboard boxes are great frame fodder and old magazines and newspapers make fabulous decorating scraps. Your materials list can be tailored to include whatever you have available. Keep in mind that sometimes it's the materials you provide that attract teens (especially boys) to a project. Have paint and embellishments on hand that will appeal to the guys in your group: toys, cars, maps, sports, bits of hardware—you get the picture.

SUPPLIES AND TOOLS

- box cutter or craft knife (for cutting cardboard)
- craft glue*
- glue sticks with glitter
- grommet setter
- hole punch
- markers
- paintbrushes*
- pencils*
- rulers*
- scissors*
- sewing needles (large, for sewing frames together, and medium-sized, for sewing on details)
- small containers for sorting
- stamps and ink pads
- stencils or scrapbook templates

MATERIALS

- assorted embellishments (glitter, beads, ribbon, sequins, jewels, small toys, stickers, hardware, etc.)
- binder clips
- brads
- cardboard (textured works well)
- craft foam sheets
- duct tape (assorted colors and patterns)
- embroidery floss
- fabric scrap
- felt
- grommets
- lacing (twine, ribbon, cord, yarn, etc.)
- magnets
- paint (acrylic, stencil, tempera, watercolor, etc.)
- paper clips
- paper scrap (old maps, magazines, weeded books, etc.)
- poster board

*One for each participant

prep work

Getting the Project Ready

Read through the whole project and make copies of the directions to give to teens at the session. If possible, make a sample (or have one made) to display.

Cut cardboard for backings into standard frame sizes (3 by 5 inches, 4 by 6 inches, 5 by 7 inches, 2½ by 2½ inches, etc.). Cut felt backings slightly smaller than the cardboard backings. Cut additional cardboard and poster board into frame shapes in corresponding sizes. You can use stencils or scrapbook templates to cut frames into fancier shapes.

Getting the Room Ready

Cover the worktable. Set wastebaskets around the table for easy cleanup. Put your sample finished frame on the table to inspire teens. For each participant, lay out pencil, ruler, scissors, a few paintbrushes, and glue. Other materials can be placed in the middle of the table, sorted into containers.

Before getting started, show the group your sample and explain the basics of the project. You may want to go over the instructions with the group, or give the teens a few minutes to read through the directions on their own and then answer any questions they may have.

directions

Read all of the instructions first!

1 Assembling the Backing

Gather the frame, cardboard backing, felt backing, and other materials you want to use. Think about how you want your frame to hang (magnets, grommets, clips, brads, etc.).

Begin by gluing the felt to the cardboard backing; the felt side is the back of your frame [a]. If you're planning to use magnets to hang your picture, attach them now. Put the backing aside.

2 Covering the Frame

This is where you let your creativity take over. You can cover the entire frame in fabric, or rip up paper scraps and glue them down. You can apply glitter in strips or paint the whole frame. The possibilities are endless. After you finish this step you can either go on to step 3 and embellish your frame or skip to step 4.

3 Embellishing

This is your chance to polish your frame. Embellishing can add layers to the design or establish a theme for your frame. Beads, ribbon, sequins, jewels, and little toys can be glued to the frame to personalize it. Use stickers, painted stencils, duct tape, or shapes cut from craft foam. Dry brushing paint can add an aged effect. Embellish to your heart's content!

4 Assembling the Frame

There are several ways to assemble your frame, so think about which one will work best for you.

- **Gluing/sewing option 1.** Glue *only* the top edge of the frame to the cardboard backing [b]. You can also sew the edges with embroidery floss or use lacing to thread the pieces together.

- **Gluing/sewing option 2.** Glue all edges *except* the top to the cardboard backing [c]. Again, you can use embroidery floss or lacing instead of glue; just be sure three edges are closed and you end up with a little pocket where you can slide in your picture.

a
Gluing felt to cardboard

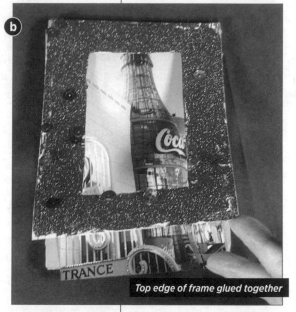
b
Top edge of frame glued together

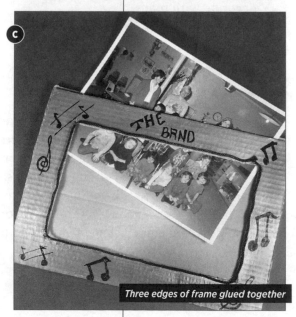
c
Three edges of frame glued together

- **Grommets.** Place a grommet in each corner of the frame **[d]**. This allows for easy hanging: just thread a piece of lacing material through the grommets.

- **Paper clips or binder clips.** Use clips to hold the frame to the backing **[e]**. They also make great hangers!

- **Brads.** Punch holes in the corners; insert brads **[f]**. Tie a piece of lacing material around the brads to hang the frame.

quick-fire version

Make up simple frames ahead of time and supply teens with easy-to-use decorating and embellishing elements. Stick with one style of frame and pre-cut, -glue, and -hole-punch as needed. Teens will still express their own style even if you limit their choices.

Provide decorating options that don't need a lot of drying time:
- markers
- glue sticks with glitter
- dry-brush stencil paint that dries quickly
- stamps and ink pads

Easy embellishing ideas:
- lace yarn or ribbon through holes punched in the frame
- decorate with brads
- sew simple patterns or shapes with yarn

adaptations

With a few additional supervisors and some adjustments in materials and supplies (fewer choices and larger frames), this project can be adapted for younger children or developmentally disabled patrons. Seniors might be interested, as well; you may want to ask them to bring in some materials from home or provide more sophisticated embellishments for them to work with.

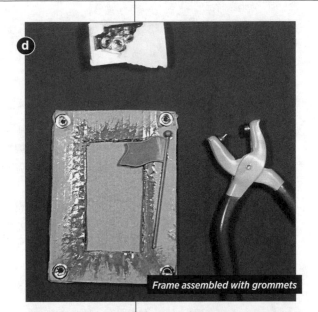

Frame assembled with grommets

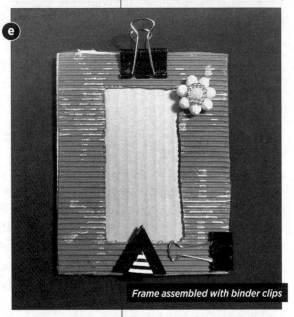

Frame assembled with binder clips

Frame assembled with brads

project 2

Difficulty:
Easy

Time:
90 minutes

Supervision:
Light–medium

Group Size:
6–8 teens per librarian

Mess Factor:
Medium

paper scrap stationery

m**AKING STATIONERY IS A GREAT WAY TO** recycle old magazines and paper scrap. Electronic age teens may balk at something as old school as stationery, but remind them that they can make custom party invitations, thank-you notes, birthday cards, valentines, note card sets to give as gifts, and more. It's environmentally friendly, easy on the teenager's budget, and of course, fun to make.

- blank envelopes of
  various sizes for
  making templates
- crayons
- glue sticks*
- lightweight cardboard
  or poster board
- markers*
- pencils and pens*
- rulers*
- scissors*
- scrapbooking scissors
- stamps and ink pads
- stencils

- blank address labels
- card stock for note cards
- paper for stationery
  sheets
- paper scrap
- stickers

One for each participant

prep work

Getting the Project Ready

Read through the whole project and make copies of the directions
to give to teens at the session. Make a few samples to display.

Go through your paper scrap to find material for envelopes. Whole
pages work best. The glossy pages of magazines and color comic books
have dynamic colors and art that are perfect for this project (although
it's not a good idea to use thin newsprint comic pages for the envelopes).

Have paper of various colors and (if possible) textures on hand. Card
stock is also good for teens who would rather make note cards.

Make envelope templates by unfolding an envelope and tracing its shape
onto cardboard or poster board, and then cutting the shape out. After you
cut it out, mark the fold lines with dotted lines, carefully fold the template
itself, or glue the blank envelope to the face of the template. It's a good
idea to have several of these templates in a variety of sizes for the teens
to pass around. Try to have at least one template for every two participants.
If your teens are relatively careful, the templates can be reused in the future.

Getting the Room Ready

Cover the worktable. Set wastebaskets around the table for easy cleanup. Display your samples. For each participant, lay out pencil, pen, marker, scissors, glue stick, and ruler. Stack envelope templates and the magazines, comics, or whatever paper scrap you're using in the middle of the table for easy access. Put your paper for stationery sheets, address labels, stamps and ink pads, and other supplies on a side table. Put a large wastebasket here also.

Before getting started, show the group your sample and explain the basics of the project. You may want to go over the instructions with the group, or give the teens a few minutes to read through the directions on their own and then answer any questions they may have.

directions

Read all of the instructions first!

1 Making the Envelopes

Go through the paper scrap and pull out a few pages you'd like to use for your envelopes **[a]**. Place the envelope template on the page, moving it around so the template fits and so the image shows up to best effect on the face of the envelope. After you've positioned the template, trace around it, and then cut along that line **[b]**. Fold into the envelope shape (using the template guides if you need to) **[c]**. Glue the side flaps down to the bottom flap **[d]**, fold the top flap over, and your envelope is complete. For a set, make 6–12 envelopes.

2 Making the Stationery

After your envelopes are done, choose paper to make your stationery pages or note cards. Measure the paper stock against your envelopes, and cut the paper to fit **[e]**.

Design your pages any way you like using stickers, stamps, stencils, or scrap paper cut and glued onto the pages. If you want, coordinate the paper with the envelopes by using matching decorations. You can

Paper scrap for envelopes

Tracing the envelope shape

Folding the envelope

Gluing the envelope flaps

also create decorative edges on your pages by ripping along the edge or using scrapbooking scissors and brushing ink from an ink pad across the edge with a tissue **[f]**.

Keep in mind that you can use the card stock to create note cards instead of stationery pages **[g]**. Embellish the cards in the same way as you would the paper. To form the card, just cut and fold the card stock to fit your envelopes. You can also leave the card unfolded: a simple nonfolded card, decorated and designed, can be quite artistic and elegant.

3 Adding Address Labels

If your envelopes are large enough to accommodate larger address labels, you can embellish these as well **[h]**. Add stamps or stickers at the edges of the label for extra flair. Just be sure to leave room to write an address.

Place a blank address label on the front of an envelope. You can put a return address label on the back flap, if desired. Now write a note or letter and send it off by snail mail. Or put together a set of your one-of-a-kind stationery for a great gift.

quick-fire version

This project is so simple that a quick-fire version is almost unnecessary. If you need to cut even more time, just have teens make fewer pieces. Or precut everything, including the envelopes, and then let teens fold, glue, and embellish.

adaptations

The project is basic enough for most groups as is. For very young kids or developmentally delayed participants, cut everything ahead of time and prefold the envelopes. This project also works very well with family groups led by a parent or older child.

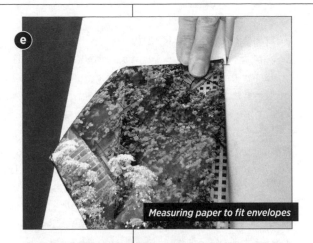
Measuring paper to fit envelopes

Sample stationery sheets

Sample note cards

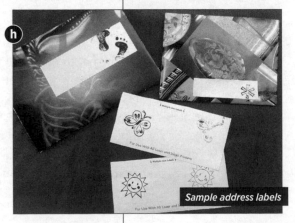
Sample address labels

design your own patches

PATCHES AND PINS HAVE LONG BEEN A FAVORITE WAY FOR teens to make statements about their likes and dislikes, right on their jackets, jeans, or book bags. Whether they feature music, BFFs, can't-miss TV shows, home teams, or favorite books, DIY patches give teens a creative way to show their colors.

This project uses recycled denim (from jeans, jackets, or skirts), which is one of the easiest fabrics to find cheap or free at your local thrift shop, if not in your closet. Teens can even bring in their own material. Just one pair of jeans yields a lot of great pieces: large back pockets, small watch pockets, and legs for cutting shapes.

After the prep work, the patches go together very quickly and easily, so you might want to give teens the option of making several. Encourage them to try different techniques and materials. Teens will enjoy doodling with fabric markers or fabric paint; making more elaborate designs with stencils or sketching; or adding embellishments such as buttons, beads, and sequins.

prep work

Getting the Project Ready

Read through the whole project and make copies of the directions to give to teens at the session. If possible, make a sample (or have one made) to display.

Prepare the denim by making sure it is clean and wrinkle free. Take the jeans apart by cutting off the legs and pockets. The back pockets of jeans lend themselves to making interesting pocket patches, so when cutting off the pockets, cut around the outside seam so the piece is still a functioning pocket. You can also use the small watch/change pockets in the same way. When cutting the legs, cut along one of the side seams in order to get the largest amount of denim.

Trace the pattern templates onto lightweight cardboard and cut them out.

When patches are finished, they can be attached by ironing on, gluing, or sewing. (There's also the nonpermanent safety pin option.) If you're short on time or equipment, you can have teens take the patches home, let them dry, and decide where they want to put them. In this case you can provide attachment instructions on a handout that you send home, so teens can attach the patches with the help of a parent.

If you plan to have the teens attach their patches during the session, we recommend you decide on one method of attachment before you begin the project. This will keep teens focused on the design. Iron-on is our favorite method.

- **Iron-on.** To prep for ironing on, cut the denim down to fit a sheet of fusible web, then follow the directions on the fusible web packaging to iron the web onto the back of the denim pieces [a]. *Do not remove the backing layer of the fusible web.* The teens will remove the backing when they are ready to iron the patch onto whatever they've decided to attach it to. After you've ironed on the web, you might want to cut the fabric down further into sizes that will be easier to work with, such as 8 by 10 inches or 4 by 5 inches.

- **Sewing.** Hand sewing is the least permanent way of attaching the patches, but it lets teens refresh their patches fairly easily. For hand sewing, show teens how to use a simple running stitch or whip stitch. (See the glossary for examples of these stitches.) You can also machine stitch the patches on if you have a machine handy and have experience sewing thicker fabrics.

- **Gluing.** Fabric glue doesn't hold well, but quick-drying glue works great. It's as easy as spreading the glue on the back of the patch and sticking the patch where you want it to go. You'll need to let the glue

SUPPLIES AND TOOLS

- fabric markers or permanent markers
- iron and towel or ironing board
- lightweight cardboard or poster board for making templates (squares, circles, triangles; see appendix A)
- metal thimbles
- paintbrushes
- pencils and pens
- pressing cloth
- quick-drying glue
- rulers
- scissors*
- sewing needles
- sponges
- stencils
- trays (plastic or Styrofoam)*

MATERIALS

- assorted embellishments (buttons, beads, sequins, ribbon, leather scraps, etc.)
- embroidery floss
- fabric paint
- iron-on fusible web
- safety pins
- scrap denim (jeans, jackets, skirts, etc.)
- thread

One for each participant

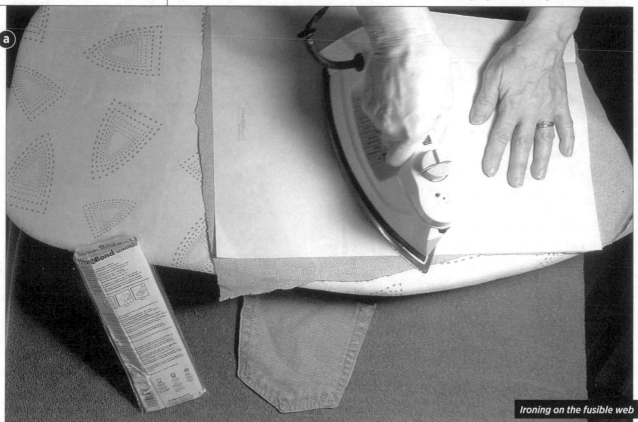

Ironing on the fusible web

dry, and you may want to weight it down with something heavy to prevent lumps.

Getting the Room Ready

Cover the worktable. Set wastebaskets around the table for easy cleanup. Display your sample patches. For each participant, lay out a tray with scissors and a piece or two of the denim and maybe a pocket. Allow plenty of room at the worktable for each teen to cut fabric. Keep the pencils, pens, fabric paint and markers, and scissors centrally located on the worktable for easy access. Lay tools and other supplies on a side table, with a large wastebasket nearby.

If you plan to iron patches on during the session, you'll need to have an iron and a towel set up on a table (or you can use an ironing board). Have the instructions from the fusible web package on hand. You'll need to decide whether you want to do all the ironing yourself or let the teens do it—with supervision, of course.

Before getting started, show the group your sample and explain the basics of the project. You may want to go over the instructions with the group, or give the teens a few minutes to read through the directions on their own and then answer any questions they may have.

directions

Read all of the instructions first!

1 Designing and Creating a Patch

Decide on the size and shape of your patch. Cut out your denim.

You can do freehand drawing or write out words. Don't be afraid to create a more abstract design with paint or markers. Think Jackson Pollack, Picasso, or even graffiti street art. If you're unsure of your drawing skills, you can sketch out your design with a pencil first.

Once you're satisfied with your creation, use permanent markers or fabric paint to fill it in **[b]**. When using the permanent markers, be aware that the fibers from the denim tend to stick to the marker tip, so you will need to wipe off the point occasionally.

If precision lines and design are more your style, try using templates or stencils. You can use markers to draw around the outlines or sponge paint on to fill in the forms **[c]**. Overlap stencils to layer your effects or create a repeating design.

Let the paint dry before embellishing. While it's drying, you can start another patch.

2 Embellishing

After your patch is dry, sew on some embellishments with a few well-placed stitches **[d]**. Use buttons, beads, sequins, or even bits of ribbon or leather, but beware of using too many extra bits— you don't want them catching on every doorway and passerby.

3 Attaching the Patch

Keep in mind that if you used fabric paint, your patch will need to dry overnight before you attach it.

- **Ironing on.** Ironing should be done by an adult or with close supervision. Be sure to read and follow the instructions from the fusible web package closely. Generally you remove the backing paper, lay the patch on the item you want to attach it to,

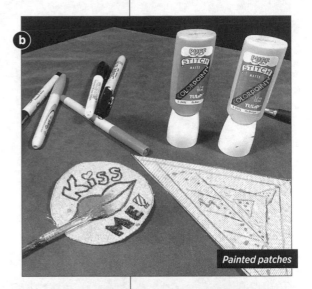

Painted patches

Stenciled patches

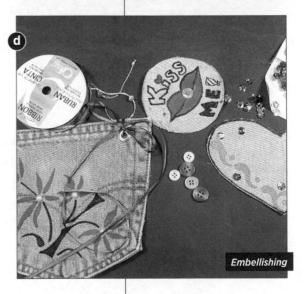

Embellishing

press the iron down firmly for about 60 seconds, and then turn the item over and press the iron on the back side for another 60 seconds. For painted patches, use a pressing cloth to cover the patch while ironing.

- **Gluing.** Spread quick-drying glue (it holds better than fabric glue) on the back of the patch and place the patch where you want it. Weight it down with something heavy to prevent lumps. Let the glue dry.

- **Sewing.** You can hand stitch your patch using a needle and thread. To further enhance the design, you can sew it in place using embroidery floss in a contrasting or coordinating color. Use a simple running stitch or whip stitch along the edge of your patch all the way around. Take your time with the sewing to make sure your stitches are straight and even.

    If your patch is a pocket, be sure not to sew the pocket closed. Also, be careful when sewing through the thick parts of the denim. If you can, place your stitches just to the inside of the existing sewn seam on the pocket **[e]**.

Sewing on the inside of the seam

quick-fire version

Prep all of the patches with the fusible web to iron on later. Precut the denim into patches so the teens can concentrate on the decorating and embellishing. Be sure to include different shapes, and have the iron-on instructions photocopied for them to take home.

For design options, stick to markers and other inks to cut down on the need for drying time. For embellishments, let teens sew things into place, as opposed to gluing.

adaptations

This project will work as is for tweens or developmentally challenged patrons. Use the quick-fire tips and have things prepped in advance. You'll probably want to offer more supervision or set it up as a collaborative project with mentors or parents.

no-sew organizers

Difficulty:
Medium

Time:
60–90 minutes

Supervision:
Light

Group Size:
8–10 teens per
librarian

Mess Factor:
Medium

mAKE COLORFUL ORGANIZERS FOR TEENS' bedrooms or school lockers with versatile and easy-to-use craft foam. It cuts easily without fraying, and it's easy to bend into different shapes. Even scraps are useful. We used mainly 11-by-17-inch foam pieces for backgrounds, trying both vertical and horizontal layouts. You could also trim it down to make an organizer to fit into a binder or scale it up to create a dynamic wall hanging. Or create some cute place mats for younger kids.

15

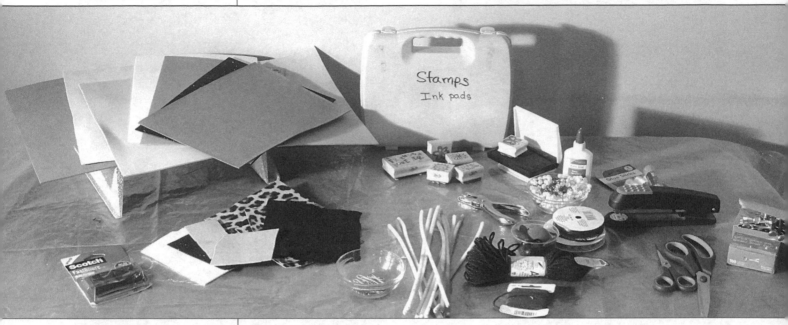

SUPPLIES AND TOOLS

- craft glue
- glue sticks
- hole punches or awls
- markers
- paintbrushes
- pencils and pens
- rulers
- scissors
- scrapbooking scissors
- stamps and ink pads
- staplers

MATERIALS

- assorted embellishments (beads, ribbon, yarn, stickers, etc.)
- brads (plain brass or fancier scrapbooking brads)
- craft foam sheets
- craft paint
- glitter craft foam (this also comes with adhesive backing)
- lacing (twine, ribbon, cord, yarn, etc.)
- paper clips, pipe cleaners, or wire
- self-stick Velcro squares (for hanging)

prep work

Getting the Project Ready
Read through the whole project and make copies of the directions to give to teens at the session. If possible, make a sample organizer (or have one made) to display.

When purchasing craft foam, make sure to get a variety of colors. If you have large and unwieldy pieces of foam, you may want to cut them down. We have listed several ways of attaching pockets to the organizers; you may choose to use only one method, or all.

Getting the Room Ready
Cover the worktable. Set wastebaskets around the table for easy cleanup. Display your sample. Place scissors, rulers, pencils, pens, hole punches, and glue on the main worktable. Arrange the rest of the materials on a side table.

Before getting started, show the group your sample and explain the basics of the project. You may want to go over the instructions with the group, or give the teens a few minutes to read through the directions on their own and then answer any questions they may have.

directions

Read all of the instructions first!

1 Designing the Organizer

Plan whether you want the finished piece to be vertical or horizontal, how many colors you want to work with, and whether you want to incorporate a theme.

Then pick the foam, fasteners, and embellishments you want to use. You will need a large piece of foam for the background piece of the organizer, as well as some smaller pieces for pockets, straps, and decorative details.

2 Making Pockets, Straps, and Other Decorations

After you've chosen your materials, set aside the piece of foam that will form the background. Then cut out your pockets and other pieces.

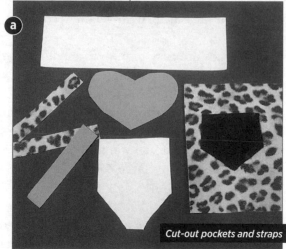
a

• **Pockets.** Think about what you might want to put in the pockets of your organizer before you cut them; this will help you decide how big they need to be. Also decide how many pockets you'd like on the finished organizer: for example, one large pocket and a couple of small ones, or a few medium pockets, or several small pockets. Pockets don't have to be square—be creative! See page 80 for some templates to get you started **[a]**. You can use scrapbooking scissors to put a distinctive edge on the pockets. Or try punching holes around the edges (saving the rounds from the holes to use as decoration, too) to make a design or to string a lace through. Once you've planned your pockets, measure, mark, and cut.

Cut-out pockets and straps

• **Straps.** Straps are useful for holding pens, pencils, lip balm, and other similarly shaped things **[b]**. Attach strips of foam to the background by first fastening down both ends and then placing brads along the length of the strap to create slots for the items you'd like it to hold. You can test the sizes of the slots by using materials on hand.

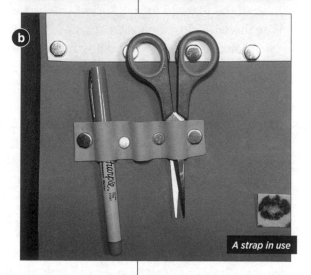
b

A strap in use

• **Decorative Elements.** Cut out foam flowers, hearts, bugs, spaceships, geometric shapes—you name it—

to make great 3-D decorations for your piece. You can embellish the pockets with foam shapes. Craft foam also takes ink well, so you can color or stamp these pieces.

After you've cut out all of your pieces, plan how you'll arrange them on the background foam **[c]**.

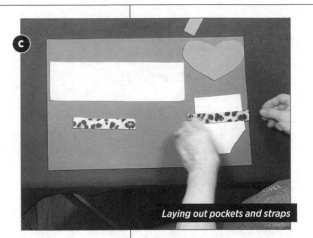
Laying out pockets and straps

3 Attaching the Pieces

Attach the pockets, straps, and decorations to your background using brads, wire, or lacing. You can use one technique or mix them up to enhance the design.

If you find the pieces are too hard to keep in place as you are attaching them, tack them in place using a glue stick. The glue is just temporary and isn't strong enough to hold the pockets permanently, but it can be used to attach little, lightweight decorations.

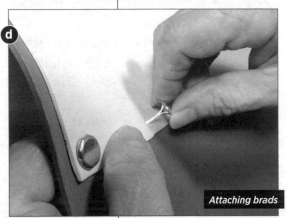
Attaching brads

- **Brads.** Brads are easy to push through the foam **[d]**. Leave them plain or decorate them with stickers or paint. Insert the brads all around the edges of the pockets (leaving the top open) **[e]**. You can measure if you want to be precise, or just eyeball the spacing. Keep in mind what you want the pocket to hold so you don't leave gaps large enough for things to slip through.

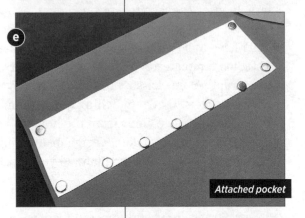
Attached pocket

- **Wire.** Another option is to poke short pieces of a small-gauge wire or small, straightened paper clips through the foam to form a sort of stitch, and then twist the wire closed on the back side. Add more visual interest by using colored wire (or paper clips) or by stringing some beads on the wire before pushing it through the foam **[f]**.

- **Lacing.** Use a lacing material like twine, yarn, or ribbon just like wire. Carefully punch holes in the foam with scissors or a hole punch or awl **[g]**, thread the twine through, and tie it in the back **[h]**. Dress up these loops with beads if you'd like. You can also punch holes around the pockets (and through the background) and lace the twine through the holes all around. Play around with the lacing pattern to see what types of designs you can come up with.

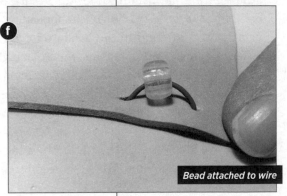
Bead attached to wire

4 Finishing

Attach small squares of self-stick Velcro to each corner of the back of your organizer, keeping the opposing pieces of the Velcro stuck together. Then peel off the remaining backings and hang the organizer where you want it.

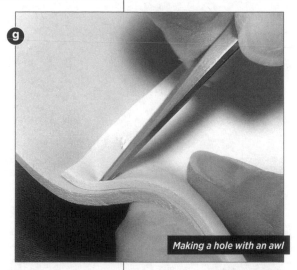
Making a hole with an awl

quick-fire version

This project is fairly easy, but if you need to save time, precut all of the pieces and let the teens focus on assembly and embellishment. Be sure to cut various colors, shapes, and sizes of pockets and straps, as well as some foam shapes for decorating. (Foam letters and shapes are available for purchase at craft stores, but it's much cheaper—and more fun—to make your own.) As another time-saver you could limit the options for attaching the elements to the background. Brads are the easiest; just make sure to have a lot of them on hand. Don't try to use glue—it is not strong enough to hold the pockets on the background.

Attaching a pocket with yarn

adaptations

This project is fun as-is for younger kids or developmentally disabled patrons. Be sure to use safety scissors and avoid using wire. This project also makes a fun parent-child activity. For adult or senior crafters, swap out the foam for more expensive backgrounds (leather or fancy felt, for example). Note that more sophisticated crafters may want a wider range of supplies, such as more elegant embellishments, sewing notions, or scrapbooking materials.

fabric scrap accessories

project
5

TEENS LOVE TO EXPRESS THEMSELVES THROUGH THEIR clothing, hairstyles, and accessories, so they might enjoy this opportunity to make their own unique pieces. While many girls will like accessory options such as hair ribbons, jewelry, bows, and so on, both boys and girls can make customized key chains, belts, and more. Materials that appeal to boys (hardware, small toys, paint) will make them feel more welcome at the craft table.

This project shows you some basic techniques to get you started making and customizing accessories. Take these basics and let your imagination run wild.

SUPPLIES AND TOOLS

- fabric markers or permanent markers
- lightweight cardboard or poster board for making templates (flower petals, hearts, bows, circles, squares, tags; see appendix A)
- masking tape
- paintbrushes
- pencils and pens
- pinking shears
- quick-drying glue
- rulers
- scissors
- sewing needles
- small containers for sorting
- stencils

MATERIALS

- assorted embellishments (buttons, beads, hardware, sequins, small toys, chain scraps, jewelry pieces, etc.)
- barrette blanks
- bar-style pin backs
- buckles or D rings
- embroidery floss
- fabric paint (including puffy and glitter)
- fabric scrap (felt, fleece, canvas, leather, suede, denim, etc.)
- key rings
- lacing (twine, ribbon, cord, yarn)

prep work

Getting the Project Ready

Read through the whole project and make copies of the directions to give to teens at the session. If possible, make a sample (or have one made) to display.

This project is ideal for using up small pieces of fabric left over from other projects. You can use denim, leather or suede, fleece, cotton—whatever you have handy. If you have larger pieces such as jeans legs or coat sleeves, take them apart and cut them into smaller pieces ahead of time. Choose fabrics with interesting patterns and colors. Lightweight fabrics work best when combined with heavier fabrics. Trace the pattern templates from page 81 onto lightweight cardboard and cut them out. If you've already tried the Design Your Own Patches project, you can have some of those on hand to use as features or embellishments.

Getting the Room Ready

Cover the worktable. Set wastebaskets around the table for easy cleanup. Display your sample accessories. Place the scissors, rulers, pencils, pens, and glue in the center of the worktable. Arrange the other materials on a side table. Sort the smaller materials into containers by type: beads, buttons, key rings, and so on. Sort the fabric scrap by weight or type of fabric. Make sure to have some lightweight cardboard on hand for teens who want to create their own pattern templates.

Before getting started, show the group your sample and explain the basics of the project. You may want to go over the instructions with the group, or give the teens a few minutes to read through the directions on their own and then answer any questions they may have.

directions

Read all of the instructions first!

1 Selecting Materials

Read through the instructions and look at the patterns and samples. The patterns are only a starting point; you may make your own patterns or do freehand designs. Decide which type of accessory you want to make so that you can narrow down your choice of materials. Then go to the materials table to choose your fabric, patterns, embellishments, and any other supplies.

2 Crafting the Pieces

Here are a few projects to try. They may kick-start your imagination and inspire you to attempt bigger, more complex pieces.

Finished layered pieces

LAYERED DESIGNS

Layering works particularly well with flowers, bows, and simple shapes (hearts, circles, etc.) [a]. You can attach this finished piece to a barrette, a hair tie, a pin, or even flip-flops or sandals. It's the most basic design, but also the most versatile. If you're feeling ambitious, cut out enough to make several items.

Choose a shape (a template or freehand creation) to layer into a stacked design [b]. Draw a few of them, varying the size and the fabric colors or textures as you like. After you've drawn or traced the shapes, cut them out of the fabric. If you like, use pinking shears to give the pieces a textured edge.

If you want, embellish the cutouts before you assemble them. For example, add dimension to your cutouts by edging them with puffy or glitter paint. Make sure to give them a few minutes to dry [c].

Next, stack the cutouts. Play around with the layering a little before you finalize it just to make sure you have the look you want. Stack the layers so they overlap in at least one spot, so that a couple of well-placed stitches can secure the entire piece. If you are making several of these, consider just pinning the layers together until your other pieces are ready to sew, and then do all the sewing at once.

Simple shapes work well for layering

Edging cutouts with glitter paint

To sew the pieces, make a few stitches through the spot where all the layers intersect using a needle and embroidery floss [d]. Add a bead or button to the center, if you want.

If you're making a bow, put a couple of stitches in the center, and then wrap the embroidery floss a few times around the center to gather the bow.

After your stitches are firmly in place, tie off the floss on the underside. Cut the ends, leaving a tail at least 2 inches long so you can tie the piece onto your accessory base [e].

Add any last embellishments or other finishing touches. Then you're ready to attach the piece to something. Use the tails of floss to tie it to a barrette, hair tie, headband, flip-flop, or anything else you can think of [f]. After you tie it, you might need to add a few spots of glue to make sure it stays in place.

You can also glue the piece to a pin back, making it a reusable attachment to almost anything.

STRANDS OF SHAPES

You can turn a finished chain or strand of shapes into a belt, a bookmark, or simple jewelry, or even tie or sew it onto a pair of sandals [g]. For this project, you'll need lacing, cut shapes, beads or other embellishments that can be strung, and glue.

Make the shapes in the same way you would for a layered piece, tracing shapes onto fabric and cutting them out. Cut at least two of each shape so that you can glue them together to make the pieces for your chain or strand.

Choose your lacing material (twine, ribbon, cord, yarn) and cut it long enough for whatever you're making—belt, headband, necklace—with enough extra length to tie the ends together. You can use more than one strand of lacing, or multiple lacing materials, to enhance the design of the piece.

Tie a large knot at one end of the lacing material, then lay it on the table, taping the knotted end down to secure it. Then string on the beads and glue on the shapes. To attach the shapes, glue two pieces together with the lacing sandwiched between [h]. As you go, add beads and knots. The pattern you create is up to you.

d Sewing layers together

e Sewn pieces with tails

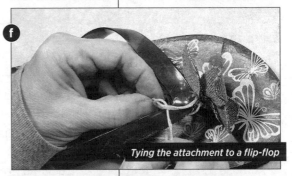
f Tying the attachment to a flip-flop

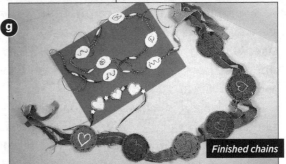
g Finished chains

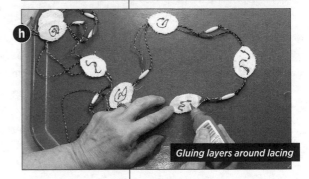
h Gluing layers around lacing

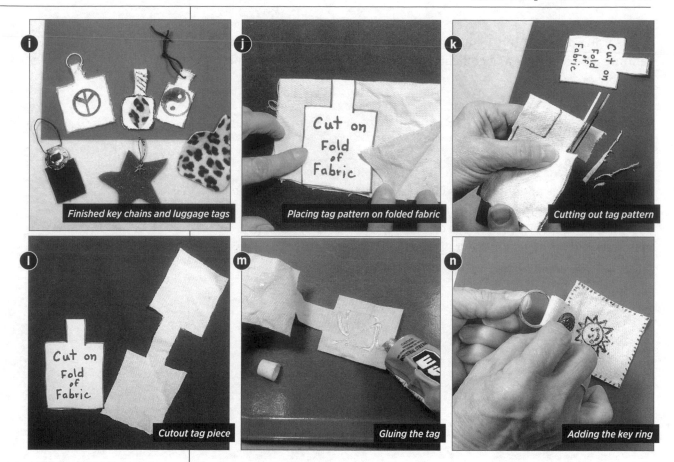

i — Finished key chains and luggage tags

j — Placing tag pattern on folded fabric

k — Cutting out tag pattern

l — Cutout tag piece

m — Gluing the tag

n — Adding the key ring

After you've made your strand and the glue has dried, feel free to go back and trim any rough edges from the shapes if you think they need it. You can also add fabric paint or sequins or any other trimmings at this point.

KEY CHAINS AND LUGGAGE TAGS

To make key chains or luggage tags, choose a heavier fabric like canvas, denim, leather, or felt [i].

Fold the fabric in half, and place the tag template so the loop end is right up against the fold [j]. Trace the shape for the tag onto the fabric.

After you've cut the fabric out [k, l], glue the layers together, leaving the loop open [m]. When the glue has dried, use paint, ink, stencils, or embellishments to decorate the tag. These tags can be mini works of art!

To finish the tag, attach a piece of sturdy cord, a carabiner, or a large key ring to the loop [n].

quick-fire version

To do a quick version of this project, choose only one technique, such as the layered attachment or key chain, for the group to do. Precut all of the pieces using different textured and colored fabrics. Have the teens concentrate on decorating and embellishing after they go through the quick assembly process.

adaptations

For younger teens or developmentally challenged patrons, stick with larger accessories and offer fewer choices. Have the group make simple shapes to use for things like bookmarks, pendants, or key chains.

To tailor this project for adults or seniors, add more sophisticated materials and allow for finer details. Include things like lace, seed beads, posh buttons, and gems.

recycled mobiles

THIS PROJECT IS IDEAL FOR GIVING TWEENS AND TEENS A way to use broken or outgrown toys. They can make the mobiles into small displays of personal history to hang in their rooms. It's a good project for partners, too; one teen can hold the mobile up while the other ties or balances the pieces.

Mobiles can add color and personality to a space without requiring any permanent changes. Consider bringing your group together to make a few to decorate your teen area. If you're very ambitious, you can even choose teams and make it a contest. (Make up rules: each mobile must use a certain number of pieces, certain items are worth more points, each team must be done in a certain amount of time, and of course, each team's mobile must be balanced.)

SUPPLIES AND TOOLS

- glue sticks
- paintbrushes
- pencils
- permanent markers
- quick-drying glue or hot glue
- scissors
- shoe boxes*
- small containers for sorting
- small drill or Dremel tool

MATERIALS

- assorted embellishments (jewelry pieces, small toys, game tokens, charms, key chains, stickers, etc.)
- craft paint
- craft sticks, dowels, or CD spools
- duct tape (assorted colors and patterns)
- jump rings
- key rings (medium or large size)
- lacing (twine, ribbon, cord, yarn, etc.)
- paper clips
- paper scrap
- recycled CDs

*One for each participant

prep work

Getting the Project Ready

Read through the whole project and make copies of the directions to give to teens at the session. If possible, make a sample (or have one made) to display.

This project is all about the materials. Choose materials teens are likely to be excited by: larger jewelry pieces like pendants or bangles and small,

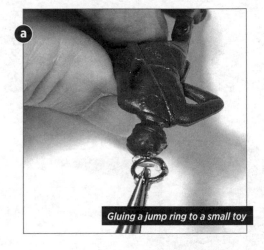

Gluing a jump ring to a small toy

lightweight toys like army men, doll parts, or game pieces. You could even have a couple of teen volunteers select and sort appropriate materials beforehand. Let teens know that they're free to bring their own materials to the session.

It's important to choose materials that can be strung. You might be surprised at how few things have convenient little holes to tie string to, especially toys. You can either use a small drill or Dremel tool to add holes or glue jump rings on the items that need attachment points [a].

Getting the Room Ready

Cover the worktable. Set wastebaskets around the table for easy cleanup. Display your sample mobile. For each participant or team, lay out a shoe box to carry their materials in and a CD spool or pair of dowels or craft sticks for their base. Put scissors, glue sticks, pencils, stringing materials, and paper clips on the worktable. Lay out the other materials on a side table. Sort similar items into small containers (for example, use separate boxes for jewelry pieces, toys, key chain, and CD spools). Ideally, you should have someplace to hang the mobiles as you're working on them. If possible, set up a temporary clothesline or use a coatrack. If the weather is nice, using a tree outside would work as well.

Before getting started, show the group your sample and explain the basics of the project. You may want to go over the instructions with the group, or give the teens a few minutes to read through the directions on their own and then answer any questions they may have.

directions

Read all of the instructions first!

1 Selecting Materials

Start by perusing the available materials. Grab things that catch your eye. You don't want to weigh your mobile down too much, so you may not be able to use everything you select, but going with your first instincts should give you a good selection to choose from. A few possible themes are army men, doll accessories or doll parts, holidays, games, books, and movies. Use one of these ideas or come up with your own.

2 Building the Base

There are two basic methods for making the base of your mobile: crossed dowels or sticks or a CD spool. Start by choosing your base.

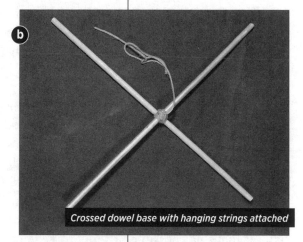

Crossed dowel base with hanging strings attached

- **Dowels or sticks [b].** Make a cross using dowels or craft sticks. Secure the pieces together by tightly wrapping them with your chosen lacing material. Tie off, leaving tails a few inches long to attach a ring for hanging. A medium or large key ring makes the perfect hanging ring. Tie the tails of the twine to the ring and secure with a few extra knots. Wrap one piece of duct tape around the junction of the sticks and another where you tied the twine to the key ring. Test the balance of your cross by holding it by the ring.

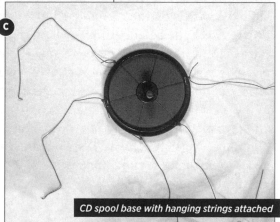

CD spool base with hanging strings attached

- **CD spool [c].** Remove the cover from the CD spool. (It can be used as a decorating or hanging element later if you'd like.) Turn the spool upside down so the spindle points down. There are holes on the spool base where the cover attaches to the base. Thread a piece of twine through each of these holes, tying it around the outside edge of the base **[d]**. You'll end up with six strings. Gather these and knot them together on the flat side of the spool, then tie them to a medium or large key ring.

Close-up of threading through holes in a CD spool

3 Embellishing the Objects

Before you attach your objects to the mobile, you may want to embellish them. Spattering red paint on doll parts makes a fabulously gory Halloween decoration. Covering CDs in festive paper can make a lovely seasonal mobile. Let your imagination run wild.

4 Assembling the Mobile

After your embellished objects are dry, you're ready to assemble your mobile. This is where having a partner comes in handy.

Cut 24-inch lengths of whatever you're using to string your mobile (twine, ribbon, yarn, etc.). You'll need as many strands as you have objects. Tie one string securely to each of your objects **[e]**. Double-knot the string and clip the end close for a clean look.

Tying a string to an object

Your pieces will hang at different lengths based on their weight. Lay your pieces out on the table, in order from heaviest to lightest, so they are easy for you to reach without the strings getting tangled **[f]**.

Begin attaching the objects to your base. If you're working in pairs, have one person hold the mobile up. If you're working alone, try to find a place to hang the base. If that's not possible, it's fine to tie your pieces while the base is on the worktable, but be sure to lift it up to check the balance after each piece.

If you're working with a crossed dowel base, you have five areas to attach objects to, and you'll need to be careful during construction so the strings don't slip off the ends **[g]**. You can use masking tape to hold the strings in place temporarily.

If you're working with a CD spool base, tie the pieces to the holes around the outside of the base and through the spindle.

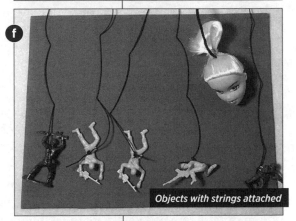

Objects with strings attached

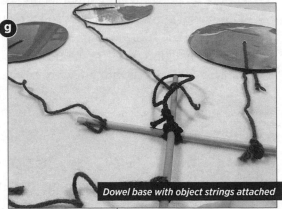

Dowel base with object strings attached

Start with the heaviest object as your center piece. This piece will have the shortest string. Tie it onto the base, leaving a long tail of string [h].

Add pieces in order of weight, working from the heaviest to the lightest, gradually lengthening the strings as you go. Remember to check the balance after adding each piece. Go back and adjust the lengths of the strings as needed to get the mobile to balance.

5 Finishing

When you're satisfied with the lengths and balance of the strings, trim each string's tail [i]. For extra security, add tape or a dab of glue to the final knots.

quick-fire version

Unfortunately, there is no good way to make this project quicker. You can have your teens work together on one large mobile for your teen area, but that won't necessarily take any less time.

adaptations

Adult crafters might like this project, but you may want to ask them to furnish their own materials (if it's a library activity) or simply give them the instructions to take home and work through on their own. It could work well to illustrate genealogy or other scrapbook or memory themes using photos and memorabilia.

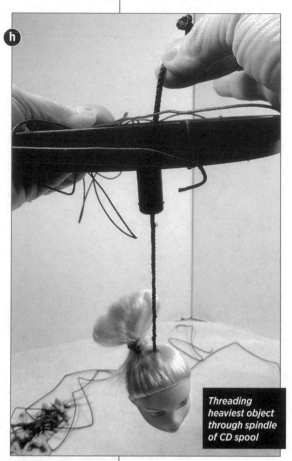

Threading heaviest object through spindle of CD spool

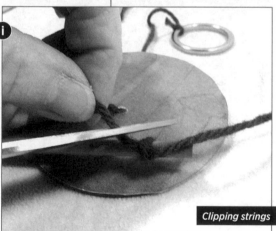

Clipping strings

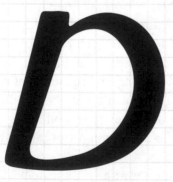
decorated containers

Difficulty:
Easy–medium

Time:
1–2 hours

Supervision:
Medium

Group Size:
6–8 teens per librarian

Mess Factor:
High

ECORATING CONTAINERS SUCH AS TINS, FLOWER-
pots, or boxes can be a flexible and creative project. You can use this project in conjunction with summer reading or book groups by offering paper scrap and embellishments related to scenes, illustrations, or text from the books; or by instructing your teens to concentrate on a specific idea or theme. This project also works well for cultural themes, seasonal displays, and gifts.

Begin by collecting mint tins, old lunch boxes, cookie tins, wooden tea boxes, candy boxes, wooden crates, coffee cans, and assorted bottles. Inexpensive containers are available at discount and dollar stores (small flowerpots, premade wooden boxes, trays, glassware, and more). You can also ask teens to bring in their own containers.

SUPPLIES AND TOOLS

- brushes (for paint and glue)*
- craft glue
- decoupage medium
- egg cartons (the Styrofoam kind)*
- hot glue
- paper towels
- pencils*
- permanent markers
- quick-drying glue
- rulers*
- scissors*
- small containers for sorting
- stencils and stencil brushes
- trays (plastic or Styrofoam)*

MATERIALS

- assorted containers
- assorted embellish- ments (beads, stones, craft marbles, small toys, jewels, ribbon, sequins, craft foam shapes, etc.)
- fabric scrap (felt, fleece, flannel, quilting squares, cotton, lace, voile, etc.)
- paint (acrylic, stencil)
- paper scrap
- small mirrors (recycled from makeup compacts or purses, or purchased)
- vellum quotes

*One for each participant

prep work

Getting the Project Ready

Read through the whole project and make copies of the directions to give to teens at the session. If possible, make a sample (or have one made) to display.

Make sure your containers are clean and dry. Cut down any fabric you're using to manageable sizes. For decoupaging fabric, choose a thin- ner fabric that doesn't fray too badly and isn't overly stretchy: cotton, lace, and sheer voile are good options. Sturdier fabrics are good for wrap- ping or lining the whole container.

Getting the Room Ready

Cover the worktable. Set wastebaskets around the table for easy cleanup. Display your sample containers. For each participant, lay out a large tray; an egg carton to use for water, decoupage, and paint; paintbrushes and glue brushes; a pencil; a ruler; and scissors. Set paint, stencils and stencil brushes, and decoupage medium in the middle of the worktable. Display your collection of blank containers on a large side table for easy selection. On this table, also arrange and sort fabric, paper scrap, embel- lishments in small containers, and other materials. If you are using hot glue, set up a separate station near an outlet, stocked with hot-glue sticks and covered with plastic or paper. Note that the hot-glue gun will require extra supervision.

Before getting started, show the group your sample and explain the basics of the project. You may want to go over the instructions with the group, or give the teens a few minutes to read through the directions on their own and then ask you questions. If you are doing this project as part of a themed program or with some other specific goal, brainstorm ideas for making your creations come to life.

directions

Read all of the instructions first!

1 Selecting and Designing a Container
Choose your container and plan your design. You can sketch patterns directly onto the container or use stencils. If you plan to paint, choose your colors. If you plan to decoupage, get the paper scrap ready by cutting or tearing it into appropriate shapes and pictures. If you plan to use fabric, cut it to size. If you want to decoupage with fabric, choose a thinner fabric that doesn't fray too badly and isn't overly stretchy. Cotton, lace, and sheer voile are good options.

2 The Base Layer(s)
Apply your base layer to the container. This process is slightly different depending on the technique(s) you decide to use.

Brushing on decoupage medium

• **Decoupage.** You can use decoupaged paper scrap or fabric for your base layer. Apply the pieces of paper or fabric that you prepared in step 1 to the surface using decoupage medium, overlapping the material to cover the entire surface. After you've covered the entire surface, go over it at least once more with the decoupage medium to seal it [a].

• **Painting.** If you use paint as your base, cover your entire container with at least one coat, even if you plan to stencil or use embellishments for your main design. If you are stenciling, you can begin adding stencils as soon as the base coat has dried [b].

During the 15–20 minutes it takes for the paint or decoupage to dry, prepare your embellishments. After the container has dried, inspect it to see if it needs another coat of paint or more fabric or paper scrap. If not, you're ready to embellish.

Stenciling

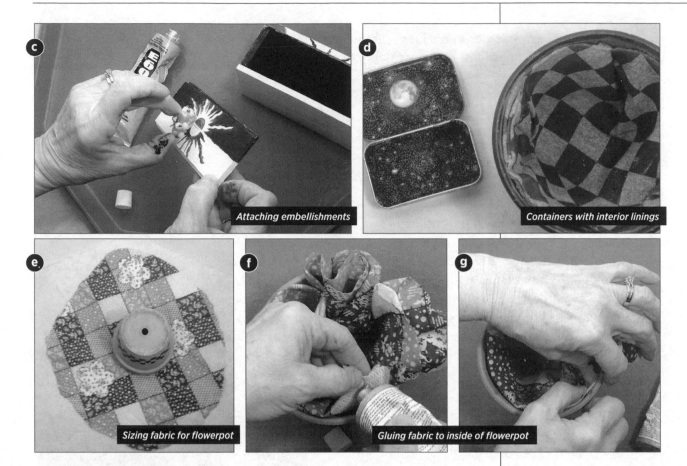

Attaching embellishments

Containers with interior linings

Sizing fabric for flowerpot

Gluing fabric to inside of flowerpot

3 Embellishing

Embellishments let you define your theme and be creative. Add some ribbon or enhance your design by outlining it in marker. You can also glue on found items, stones, craft marbles, jewels, and sequins **[c]**. Add words from text paper scrap, apply vellum quotes, or write your own words with marker or paint. Add layers of embellishments until you are satisfied with your creation. For heavier embellishments, use hot glue (with supervision) or quick-drying glue.

4 Decorating the Interior

While decorating the inside of your container is not necessary, it's a really nice finishing touch. You can paint or decoupage the inside. Using a fabric liner is a bit more challenging. Flowerpots and larger tins are easier, but with patience and careful measuring, you can line even small containers **[d]**.

To line a flowerpot, cut a circle of fabric 4–6 inches bigger than the top of the flowerpot **[e]**.

Fold the raw edge of the fabric and glue to the inner rim of the pot using quick-drying glue or hot glue **[f, g]**. Push the fabric into the bottom of the pot. For a more finished look, add a piece of ribbon around the inner rim.

To line a box or flat tin, cut a nonfraying fabric such as felt, fleece, or flannel to the size of the top or bottom of the box and glue it in place with quick-drying glue **[h]**. If your edges look ragged, glue a piece of ribbon over them **[i]**.

Another way to enhance the interior is to glue small mirrors to the top or bottom.

quick-fire version

To simplify this project, paint containers for your group ahead of time with a nice base coat of paint. If you need to make it very simple, prepare the same type of container for all of your teens, like all flower-pots or all cookie tins.

Give each teen a prepainted container along with easy embellishing items like markers and stencils, jewels or sequins, foam letters or shapes, ribbon, and plenty of quick-drying glue for attaching things.

adaptations

This project would work well for parent-child groups, even with younger children if parents are on hand for extra supervision and help. Adults or seniors would also enjoy this project with more sophisticated materials. Because the project is so flexible, you may want to consider teaming up different groups, such as teens and seniors or developmentally disabled patrons.

Gluing fabric to bottom of box

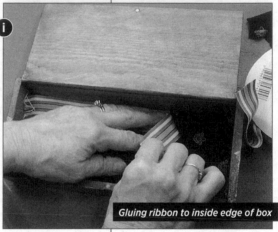
Gluing ribbon to inside edge of box

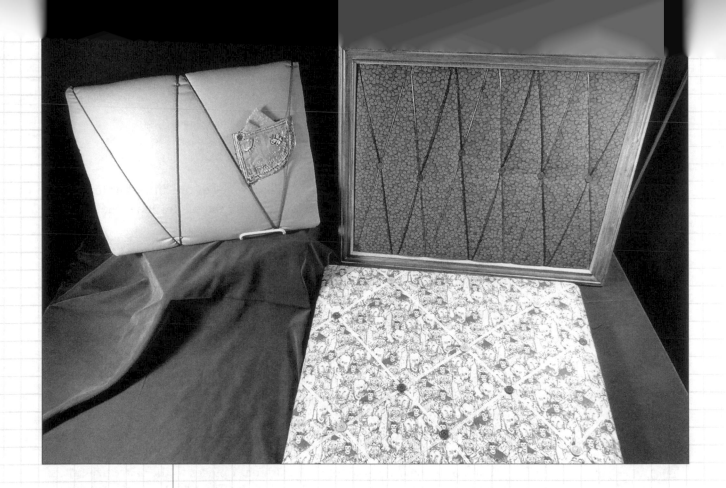

memory boards

Difficulty:
Medium

Time:
60 minutes

Supervision:
Medium

Group Size:
2–4 teens per
librarian

Mess Factor:
Medium

m**EMORY BOARDS AND PERSONALIZED BUL-**
letin boards can brighten up a room with
a splash of color and creativity. Teens can
make them as gifts or to use as their own
personalized decor. Likewise, you can make
them for displays in any of your library areas
that need a little flair. Making a funky memory board for the teen area (or better yet,
letting your teens make a few) will give you a place to showcase photos of your
regulars, or a fun place to announce goings-on for your teen groups.

   Although you can buy premade memory boards at a store, making your own can
reflect your style and interests and is cheap, easy, and fun! Beyond fabric colors
and textures, your choice of ribbon or other lacing options for the straps of the
board add depth to a design. Embellishments can pull a theme together. Finally,
finish your board with a funky recycled picture frame to create a unique result.

SUPPLIES AND TOOLS

- box cutter or craft knife (for cutting cardboard)
- flathead screwdriver
- hammer and small nails (only if adding picture frame)
- large ruler or straightedge
- large sewing needles
- masking tape
- metal thimbles or a flat stone, brick, or block of wood to push needle through board
- pencils
- pliers (for removing wayward staples)
- quick-drying glue
- scissors
- staple gun and heavy-duty staples (or regular staplers)

MATERIALS

- assorted embellishments (large buttons, jewels, charms, miniatures, pins, badges, jewelry pieces, small toys, etc.)
- batting
- cardboard (thicker corrugated cardboard is better)
- embroidery floss
- fabric (heavy cotton, denim, medium- to heavy-weight knit or flannel, upholstery fabric)
- lacing (twine, ribbon, cord, yarn, leather straps, etc.)
- large picture frames (optional)
- picture hangers (only if adding picture frame)

prep work

Getting the Project Ready

Read through the whole project and make copies of the directions to give to teens at the session. If possible, make a sample (or have one made) to display.

Decide what type of memory board you're going to make. If you're dealing with a large group or are doing the project for the first time, just make the board itself and don't worry about the picture frame. Cut the cardboard, fabric, and batting ahead of time to allow teens to focus on assembly and decorating.

When choosing fabric, stay away from sheer fabrics or anything that stretches or frays. You may be able to get brocades to work if you are very careful. Recommended fabrics are heavy cottons, upholstery fabric (provided it's not too prone to fraying), denim, medium- to heavy-weight knits (not too stretchy), and flannels. Be sure to choose fabrics that will appeal to teens, including some solid colors and some boy-friendly patterns (for example, camouflage).

For a basic board, cut all of your cardboard pieces to the same size [a]. Boards can be whatever size and dimensions you'd like, but a good size is 18 by 18 inches. The cardboard should be sturdy. If you only have thin cardboard available, you'll have to use more than one layer. You'll need one piece of cardboard per participant, but it's a good idea to have a few extras on hand just in case.

Batting is available in rolls from craft and sewing supply stores, and even some big-box stores. If you don't have very many teens, however, you can purchase it by the yard. Each board needs at least two layers of batting, but cut some extras in case some teens want thicker padding. Cut the batting to the same size as the cardboard. It doesn't have to be exact or perfectly straight, so simply lay a piece of the cardboard on the batting and cut around it [b].

Cut the fabric pieces at least 3 inches larger than the cardboard all the way around. If you are using fabric that frays, add an extra inch. As with the batting, your cuts don't need to be perfect [c].

If your group is large, you'll probably want more than one staple gun. You can supply regular staplers if you have concerns about your teens using a staple gun; however, the finished product will not be as sturdy. Alternately, a supervising adult can do the stapling for the teens.

You don't need to precut the materials for the straps of the boards, but have plenty of fun and creative choices on hand, such as ribbon of various widths, textures, and colors; yarn; twine; and leather cord or straps.

The traditional embellishment for memory boards is buttons, so definitely have some on hand. Also offer pins and badges, jewelry pieces, small toys, and so on.

Adding picture frames is definitely a plan-ahead option, but they are worth the trouble. Framed memory boards look fantastic and make great gifts. To make picture frame memory boards, look for medium- to large-sized frames at thrift stores or garage sales (don't be deterred if they still contain art—you can remove it). Look for frames that are about 11 by 17 inches; the frames don't need to be all the same size or shape. Remove any art from the frames and look over the frames carefully for hazards like large splinters or old staples. Cut cardboard backings to fit each frame **[d]**.

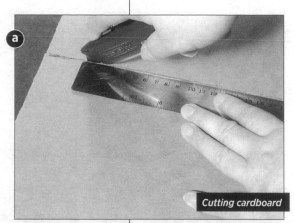

Cutting cardboard

Getting the Room Ready

Cover the worktable. Set wastebaskets around the table for easy cleanup. Display your sample board. This is an easy project, it but requires a fair amount of work space. Make sure you have enough table space for teens to spread out. Set up all of the supplies on a side table, but keep the staple guns or staplers on the main table.

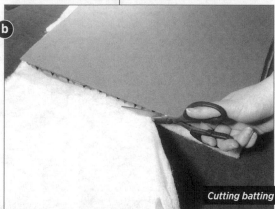

Cutting batting

Before getting started, show the group your sample and explain the basics of the project. You may want to go over the instructions with the group, or give the teens a few minutes to read through the directions on their own and then answer any questions they may have.

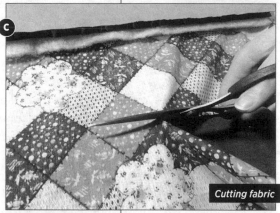

Cutting fabric

directions

Read all of the instructions first!

1 Designing the Memory Board

Choose your fabric. With patterned fabric, keep scale in mind. Big, busy patterns don't work well for smaller boards, but may be perfect for a wall-sized board. You need one piece for the face of the board and one for the back. You may want to use a solid color for the back.

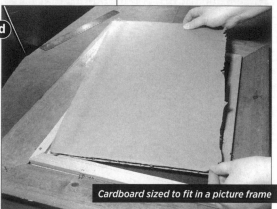

Cardboard sized to fit in a picture frame

Select the ribbon, cord, leather straps, or yarn to use for the straps of the board. You can fashion a diamond pattern, squares, or large X in the center. Play with the straps to see what you like best.

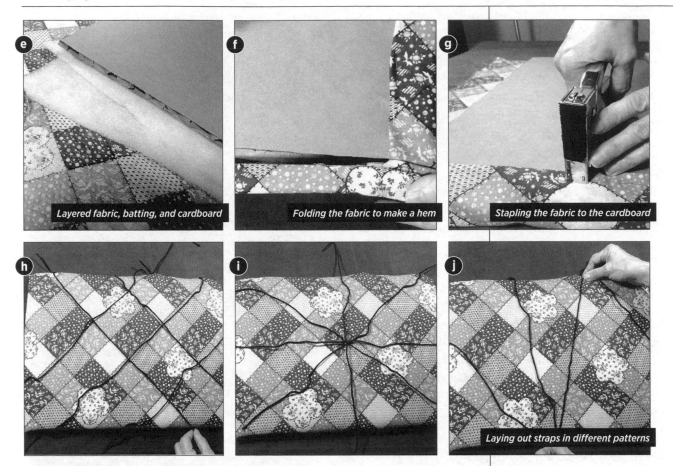

Layered fabric, batting, and cardboard

Folding the fabric to make a hem

Stapling the fabric to the cardboard

Laying out straps in different patterns

2 Building the Board

To build the board, lay your main fabric face down on the table. Then put down at least two layers of batting (or more if you want the board to be extra plush). Top off the stack with the cardboard **[e]**. Center your stack so there is an equal amount of fabric on each edge.

3 Stapling the Fabric

Pull the fabric tightly around the edges of the cardboard, folding the fabric under to create a hem **[f]**, and begin stapling it to the cardboard **[g]**. Again, fabrics that fray need a wider hem. If you find that the staples are going all the way through the board and the fabric at the front, you can use the tip of a flathead screwdriver to carefully bend the points of the staples down; just make sure the points are under the top layer of fabric and not visible. This isn't an issue that happens every time, and it can normally be avoided by using a staple gun and stapling against a hard surface.

4 Adding the Straps

Once you've decided on a design for the straps **[h, i, j]**, put them on the board (use masking tape to hold them in place, if necessary); then turn it over to staple them to the back of the board **[k]**.

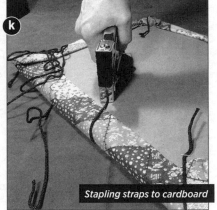

Stapling straps to cardboard

5 Sewing and Embellishing the Board

After you've stapled all the straps, turn the board back over and use embroidery floss to sew through the layers where the straps intersect **[l]**. Sewing through the straps gives the board an upholstered look as well as providing extra tension on the straps to make sure photos and such don't slip out.

Use a large, sharp needle with an eye big enough for embroidery floss. Be careful pushing it through the cardboard and other layers. Don't rush. Use a metal thimble or a block of wood to push the needle through without hurting yourself **[m]**. Put three or four stitches through each intersection of straps to make it secure. If you're adding buttons as embellishment at the intersections, you should sew those on now also.

Now you're ready to embellish and personalize your board. Glue embellishments like jewels, miniatures, or toys into place **[n]**; sew on charms or extra buttons; or decorate with pins and badges. If you're adding a frame, skip to step 7.

6 Finishing the Board

Lay your board face down on the table, then take your second piece of fabric and center it on the back of the board. Fold the edges under and staple the fabric in place, making sure to keep the fabric taut **[o]**. After you've stapled all around the edge of the board, add a piece of ribbon across the top for hanging. Staple the ribbon on very securely, and make sure it's strong enough to support the weight of the board **[p]**.

Pushing the needle through the cardboard

Sewing on a button using a wooden block to push through the layers

Attaching an embellishment with glue

Stapling back fabric to board

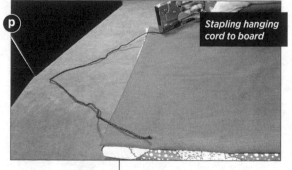

Stapling hanging cord to board

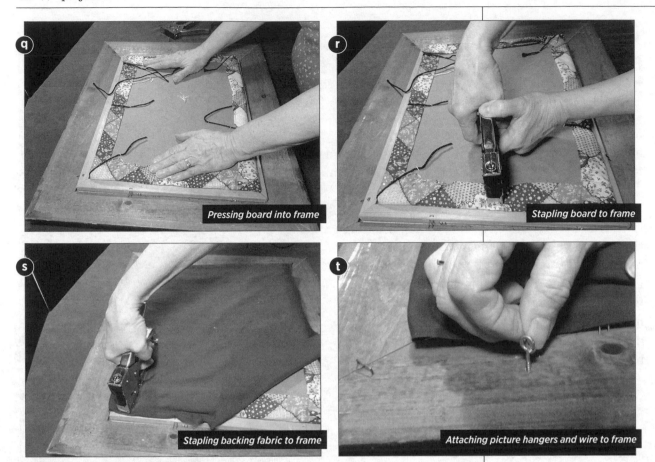

Pressing board into frame

Stapling board to frame

Stapling backing fabric to frame

Attaching picture hangers and wire to frame

7 Adding a Picture Frame

The cardboard was cut to fit the frame before assembly, so now you just need to push the board into the frame **[q]**. It may be a tight fit, but that's good because it needs to be secure. Check to see if the board wiggles at all inside the frame. If it does, staple it along the edges **[r]**. You may only need to staple in a few places—you just want to make sure the board doesn't move inside the frame.

Lay your backing fabric on the frame and staple it into place around the edges **[s]**. Then add picture hangers at the top edge of the frame **[t]**.

quick-fire version

Cut all the cardboard and batting to 11 by 17 inches. Precut all of your fabric pieces to 17 by 34 inches. Precut lengths of ribbon or cord to 20 inches and limit embellishment to large, preferably 2-hole (but still colorful) buttons.

During assembly, have the teens position the batting on the cardboard and tape it in place with masking tape (just to keep it from moving around under the fabric). Then the board-batting piece should be positioned in the center of the fabric [u].

Fold the fabric around the board so you have a seam down the center back. Tuck the ends under to make a folded hem both at the seam and along the top and bottom [v, w]. Staple the seam at the top and bottom [x]. Then for a little more stability, sew a quick X stitch at the center of the seam to keep the fabric from gaping [y].

Have the teens add straps and embellishments as in the regular instructions.

adaptations

This makes a nice parent-child project for younger kids (9- to 12-year-olds); if you want to do a library program for this age group, just use the quick-fire instructions. It would also be a good project to complement family reading during a summer reading program; families could use the boards to showcase reading lists and awards.

Placing cardboard and batting on fabric

Folding fabric around cardboard

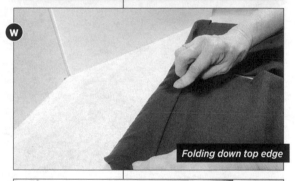

Folding down top edge

Stapling down center seam

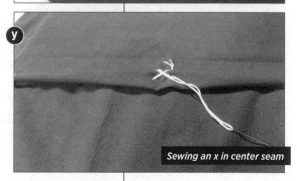

Sewing an x in center seam

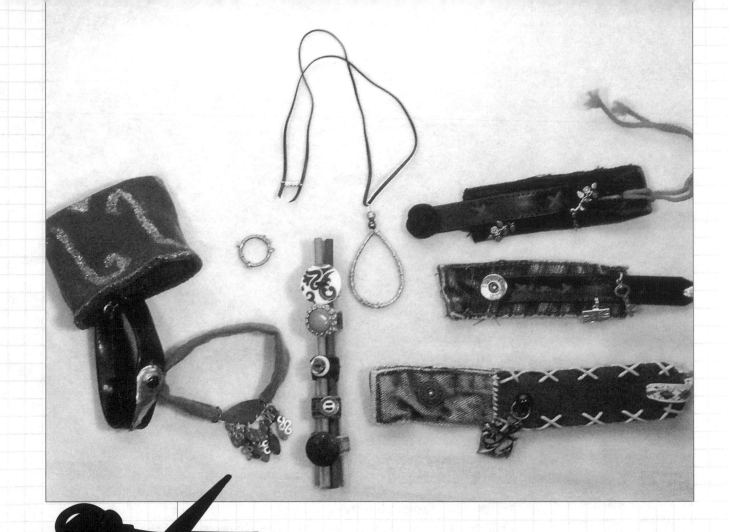

rock star jewelry

Difficulty:
Medium

Time:
60–90 minutes

Supervision:
Medium

Group Size:
4–6 teens per
librarian

Mess Factor:
Medium

GIVE TEENS A CHANCE TO LET OUT THEIR INNER GAGA BY making their own jewelry. Leather, lace, fabric, denim, old jewelry, keys, toys—almost anything can be incorporated into these little wearable works of art.

Use recycled objects with a few supplies from a craft store for this project. You can use different materials depending on the group. Try gothic pieces and lots of black lace for your *Twilight* reading group, or bits and bobs of computer hardware (small, of course) for your Teen Tech Week projects.

Belt loops are perfect for making fabric rings, and teens can quickly make enough to decorate all of their fingers and even a couple of toes. Key rings wrapped in small-gauge jewelry wire are another fun option. Or teens may opt to make fabric scrap cuffs and bracelets.

SUPPLIES AND TOOLS

- fabric markers or permanent markers
- grommet setter
- hole punch or awl
- iron and towel or ironing board
- jewelry or needle-nose pliers
- large sewing needles
- metal thimbles
- paintbrushes
- pencils and pens
- scissors

MATERIALS

- assorted embellishments (buttons, ribbon, lace, beads, keys, hardware, small toys, charms, buckles, etc.)
- embroidery floss
- fabric paint
- fabric scrap (waistbands and belt loops from jeans and pants, cuffs from shirts)
- grommets
- iron-on fusible web
- jewelry wire (assorted colors)
- jump rings
- key rings (assorted sizes)
- recycled jewelry (including pendants and other pieces, chains, hoop earrings in various shapes)
- scrap leather (from belts, purse straps, or shoes)
- sew-on snaps
- thread
- toggle closures
- twine, ribbon, cord, or yarn

prep work

Getting the Project Ready

Read through the whole project and make copies of the directions to give to teens at the session. If possible, make a sample (or have one made) to display.

Rock star jewelry pieces use a narrow band of fabric as the base. Your regular supply of fabric scrap should provide a lot of good options. Waistbands and belt loops from jeans and pants and cuffs from shirts are all ideal for this project. Scraps of leather are also very useful and can be reclaimed from belts and purse straps. Leather shoes and boots have great details like little straps, buckles, built-in grommets, and more. It takes extra time to disassemble them, but it's worth the effort; and there's something fun and cathartic about taking things apart. You can get some of your teens to help with the deconstructing process, if you'd like. Make sure everything is clean before you start deconstructing. Toss the clothing in the laundry and wipe down the leather items with a damp cloth.

Getting the Room Ready

Cover the worktable. Set wastebaskets around the table for easy cleanup. Display your sample pieces. Place scissors, pencils, pens, sewing needles, thimbles, and other tools on the worktable, and the other materials on a side table.

Before getting started, show the group your sample and explain the basics of the project. You may want to go over the instructions with the group, or give the teens a few minutes to read through the directions on their own and then answer any questions they may have.

directions

Read all of the instructions first!

RINGS: BELT LOOP

All you need is a belt loop scavenged from a pair of pants and a pretty button.

1 Sizing the Loop
Wrap your belt loop around your finger in order to measure it [a]. Use a pen to mark the length, and then cut the loop down to size.

2 Sewing the Ring
Use a needle and thread to sew the loop closed to make a ring [b]. You want the stitching to be very secure so the ring will hold up to being put on and taken off, so pull your stitches tight and go over the seam two or three times.

3 Adding the Bling
Now sew your button onto the loop, covering the seam [c]. Consider using thread, embroidery floss, or even yarn in a contrasting color to sew on the button. After the button is attached, your ring is done.

RINGS: WIRE-WRAPPED

For this ring you'll need a key ring, wire, a few small embellishments, and patience.

1 Wrapping the Ring
Find a key ring that will fit your finger [d] and choose your wire. Unwind a lot of wire. Wrapping a ring uses more wire than you'd think, and it's better to have too much than too little. You can add another piece in the middle, but you will not have as polished a look as if you use a single piece of wire for the whole ring.

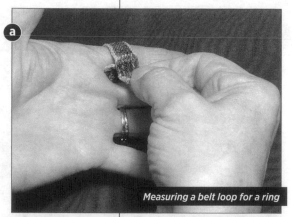
Measuring a belt loop for a ring

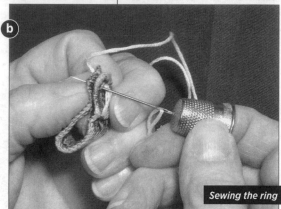
Sewing the ring

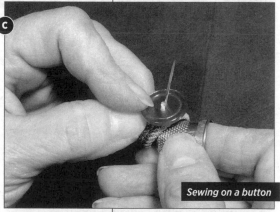
Sewing on a button

Fitting a key ring on your finger

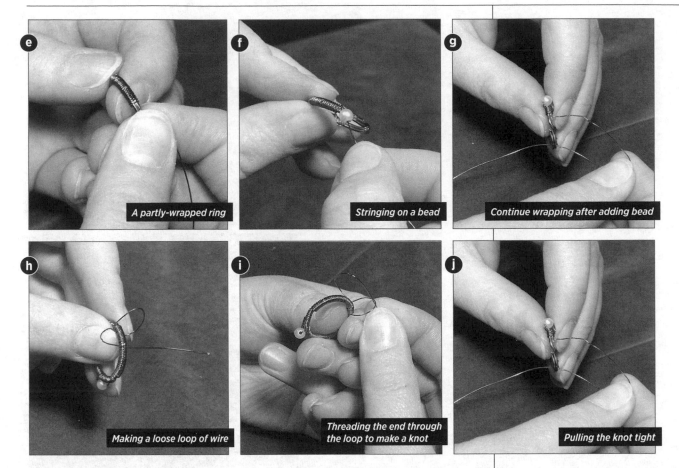

e — A partly-wrapped ring

f — Stringing on a bead

g — Continue wrapping after adding bead

h — Making a loose loop of wire

i — Threading the end through the loop to make a knot

j — Pulling the knot tight

Leaving a half-inch tail of wire, wrap a few loops of wire around the ring [e]. Then secure the end by continuing your wrapping over the tail. Continue wrapping the wire, keeping your loops tight and close together. This takes a lot of patience. If you prefer, you can use needle-nose or jewelry pliers for this.

2 Embellishing

You can add small beads or charms to your ring by threading them onto the wire as you wrap it [f]. To keep the ring comfortable to wear, use only small items. After the bead or charm is snug against the ring, wrap the next loop around the bead to secure it before you continue wrapping the wire around the ring [g].

3 Finishing

After you have wrapped your entire ring, you'll need to tie the wire off so it stays in place and so the end won't poke you. Make a loop around the ring but don't pull it all the way taut [h]. Pull the tail end of the wire under the loop so you have a knot [i], and then use pliers to pull the loop tight and work it into the wrapped coils [j]. Go through this knotting process twice to make sure your wire is secure. Clip off any excess, and you're done.

Attaching a jump ring to a charm

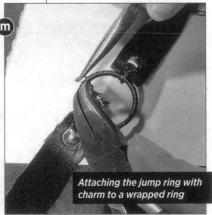

Attaching the jump ring with charm to a wrapped ring

Necklace materials

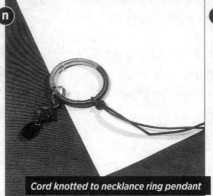

Cord knotted to necklance ring pendant

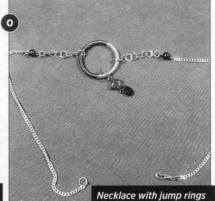

Necklace with jump rings

NECKLACES: WIRE-WRAPPED

If you like the wire-wrapped look, you can use the same method to make a pendant for a necklace.

1 Wrapping the Key Ring

Select and wrap your key ring the same as you would to make a ring, as described on page 50. Larger key rings and other open shapes (such as hoop earrings, bangles, etc.) work well for necklaces, since they don't have to fit around your finger [k].

2 Embellishing

As with the finger ring, you can add beads and charms to the wrapped necklace ring. You can either incorporate the embellishment into the wrapping or attach it after the wrapping is finished by fastening the embellishment to a small jump ring [l] and linking it to the wrapped key ring [m].

Depending on the size and type of embellishment you're working with, this may take some finessing. Be patient and work carefully. Use pliers if you need to.

3 Adding the Chain or Cord

After you have decorated your necklace ring, attach chain or cord so you can wear the ring as a necklace.

To hang the wrapped ring like a pendant, thread the cord through it and knot the cord [n]. Or add a jump ring to the wrapped ring and thread your chain or cord through that. Or attach two jump rings, and then attach the chain or cord to either side [o].

You can get creative with the type of material you use to hang your necklace. Recycled chain is nice, as is simple black cord, but you can also try ribbon, leather cord, or twine. You can even mix and match these for a unique and textural look.

CUFFS AND BRACELETS: SHIRT CUFFS

For this project, use shirt cuffs, a needle and thread, and some embellishing materials.

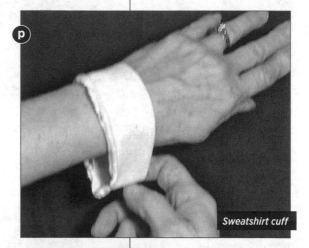
Sweatshirt cuff

1 The Base

For this style of wrist cuff you will need some shirt cuffs. These can be stretchy cuffs from sweatshirts, the sleeve hems from T-shirts, or even button-up cuffs from dress shirts.

Wrap the cuff around your wrist to measure it **[p]**. You may need to cut some of the length out, and depending on the style, the cuff may require some quick hand stitches.

If you're using sweatshirt or T-shirt cuffs, just cut off the excess material and sew the cuff closed again **[q]**. The stretchiness of the fabric should leave you enough give to slide the cuff over your hand easily.

If you're using the buttoned cuff from a dress shirt, cut the fabric out of the middle so the button and buttonhole are left intact. Sew the cut ends together. If you want the seam to be less visible, turn the cuff inside out before sewing.

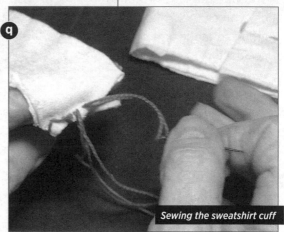
Sewing the sweatshirt cuff

2 Embellishing

Your embellishment opportunities for these cuffs are almost limitless **[r]**:

- Use fabric paint to paint a design.
- Sew on charms, beads, or buttons, randomly or in patterns.
- Sew on pendants or pieces of recycled jewelry chain.
- Sew on cord or straps of leather.
- Sew or iron on ribbon or lace using a few stitches or iron-on fusible web (and your iron).

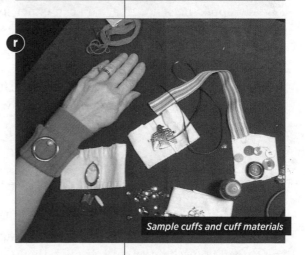
Sample cuffs and cuff materials

**CUFFS AND BRACELETS:
DENIM AND LEATHER**

For this style of cuff, use jeans waistbands, ribbon, scrap leather (from belts, purse straps, or shoes), a sharp needle and embroidery floss, a hole punch or awl to punch through the leather, and embellishments (buckles, jewelry pieces, buttons, etc.).

1 Making the Base

The base of this cuff uses the waistband button from a pair of jeans. (If you don't have the button part of the waistband, you can use a plain piece of the band and add a button to one end.)

Cut off the button end of the waistband. This piece should be about 1½–2 inches long or so (depending on the size of your wrist).

Next, choose a piece of scrap leather, either a plain piece of strap or one with a buckle. This section should be about 1½–2 inches long (measure while buckled if using a buckle piece) **[s]**. If you pick a piece with a hole or grommet, it will save you the step of punching a hole yourself.

Carefully sew the leather strap to the denim with embroidery floss **[t]**. Use a metal thimble to push the needle through. Take your time, and don't hurt your-self. You may need to work the needle through the leather and the denim layers one at a time, but you only need a few stitches so it shouldn't take too long. If you feel like getting fancy, make X-shaped stitches.

Use the hole punch or awl to make a hole at the end of the leather strap (if there isn't one there already) **[u]**. Then take a piece of ribbon about 4–5 inches long, fold it in half, and thread the folded end through the hole, passing the loose ends through the loop so the ribbon is attached to the strap **[v]**. Tie a regular knot at the other end of the ribbon to make another loop that will hitch over the button and close the cuff **[w]**.

2 Embellishing

Embellish your cuff by sewing on jewelry pieces or beads. You can also decorate with fabric paint, buttons, or lace, or mix and match. Add jump rings and charms, or badges, pins, or patches. You can even use a fabric or permanent marker to draw or write on the denim if you'd like.

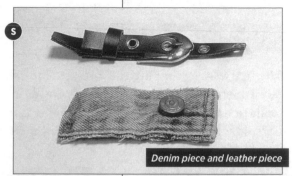
Denim piece and leather piece

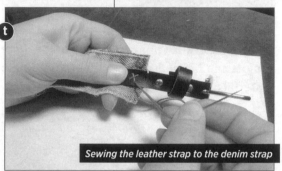
Sewing the leather strap to the denim strap

Punching a hole in the leather strap

Attaching the ribbon to the leather strap

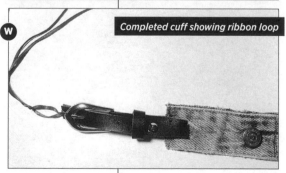
Completed cuff showing ribbon loop

quick-fire version

The best way to simplify this project is to choose one piece for teens to make. Belt-loop rings are fast and easy, as are shirt-cuff bracelets. If you want to do necklaces, the wire wrapping is the most time consuming part, so wrap a bunch of rings ahead of time (or have teens do it).

adaptations

To adapt this for younger kids, provide more direct supervision. This project can be made a lot of fun for adult crafters by providing fancier materials.

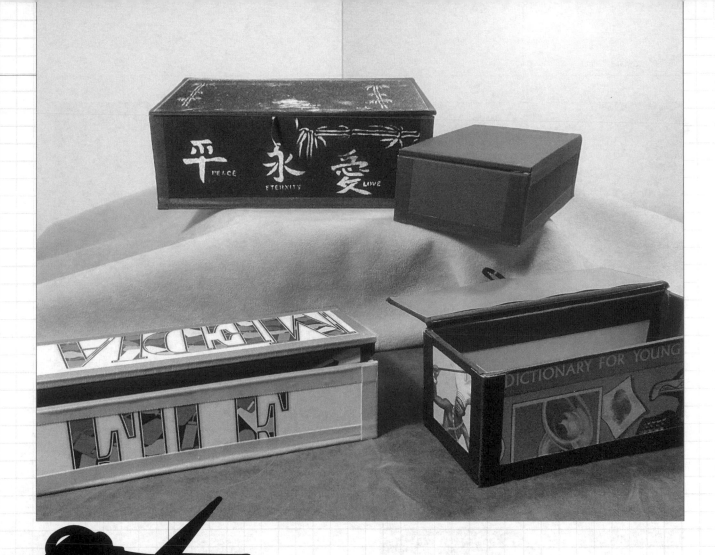

Difficulty:
Medium
(recommended
for teens 16
and older)

Time:
60–90 minutes

Supervision:
Medium–heavy

Group Size:
2–4 teens per
librarian

Mess Factor:
Medium

book boxes

CREATE FUN AND WHIMSICAL BOOK BOXES FROM HARD-cover books that have been pulled from circulation. The subject of a book can suggest the purpose of the box; for example, put seed packets in a box made from a garden-ing book, or stash candy in a box made from *The Hunger Games.* The boxes make great gifts, especially when filled with something fun.

Working this project into your programming schedule may depend on the hardcovers you have on hand. Recycling is an obvious theme, but you can tie book boxes into Banned Books Week, summer reading programs, Teen Read Week, or any of your regular campaigns.

This project requires teens to focus and plan well. We recommend it for older teens because of the cutting, although you can use it with younger teens if you do more of the prep work yourself. Measuring needs to be fairly precise so that the pieces of the box fit together well, so patience is required.

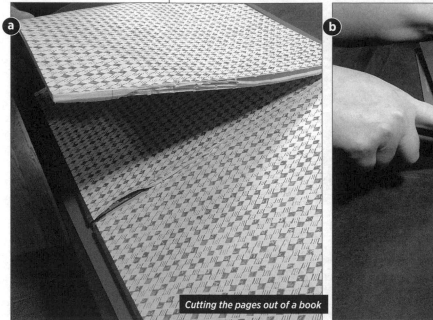

Cutting the pages out of a book

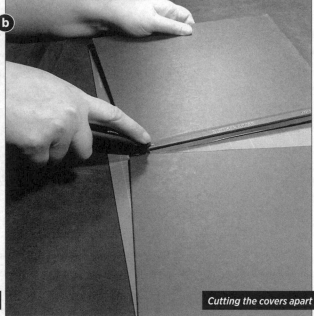

Cutting the covers apart

SUPPLIES AND TOOLS

- box cutter or craft knife
- cardboard or cutting mats
- craft glue
- metal ruler
- paintbrushes
- pencils
- scissors
- stamps and ink pads
- stencils

MATERIALS

- assorted embellishments (glitter, buttons, beads, ribbon, etc.)
- colored paper
- craft paint
- duct tape or gaffers tape (assorted colors and patterns)
- felt
- hardcover books

prep work

Getting the Project Ready

Read through the whole project and make copies of the directions to give to teens at the session. If possible, make a sample (or have one made) to display.

Carefully cut the pages out of the retired books and separate the front and back covers from the spine [a]. You can keep the pages for paper scrap for other projects, if you'd like. Wipe down the covers with a lightly damp towel to make sure they are clean.

If you don't trust your group to cut the covers, do the cutting for them [b]. Covers can sometimes be very difficult to cut, and some teens may be intimidated by the box cutter. But if your teens are willing and able, it's fine to let them do it as long as you're nearby to supervise.

Getting the Room Ready

Cover the worktable with your regular drop cloth, and then put down cardboard or cutting mats. Set wastebaskets around the table for easy cleanup. Display your sample book box. Put book covers, box cutters, rulers, and duct tape in the center of the worktable. Set glue and embellishments on a side table, and when your group gets to the decorating step you can move them to the worktable for easy access.

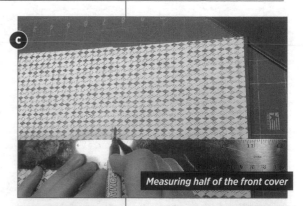

Measuring half of the front cover

Before getting started, show the group your sample and explain the basics of the project. You may want to go over the instructions with the group, or give the teens a few minutes to read through the directions on their own and then answer any questions they may have.

directions

Read all of the instructions first!

1 Cutting the Cover

You'll need to cut each cover of the book into three pieces to make the six parts of the box. First split the front cover: measure and mark a line at the halfway point on the inside of the cover [c]; then use the box cutter to cut along this line [d]. One piece will be the lid of your box.

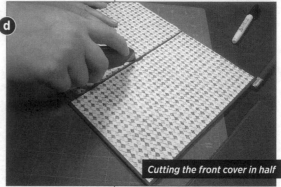

Cutting the front cover in half

Now split the remaining piece of the front cover. Measure and mark the halfway point. Make a line and cut again. Use these two pieces as the front and back of your box [e].

Repeat these actions with the back cover. This will give you the bottom of your box and pieces for the two sides. Finally, trim the side pieces so that they are about ¼ inch shorter than the side edge of the bottom piece. This way, when you assemble the box, the side pieces will fit between the front and back pieces.

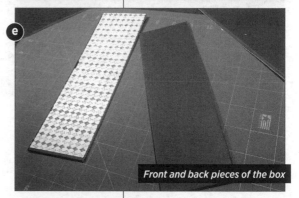

Front and back pieces of the box

2 Assembling the Box— Taping the Sides

Lay your box pieces out as shown to make sure everything will fit together as neatly as possible [f].

Begin the taping process by attaching the front piece to the bottom piece. Measure a piece of tape as long as the front piece. Place the tape along the outside edge of the front piece, leaving at least half the width of the tape hanging over the edge [g].

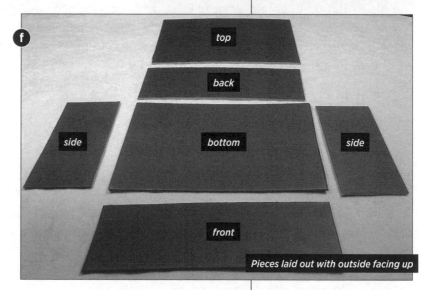

top

back

side   bottom   side

front

Pieces laid out with outside facing up

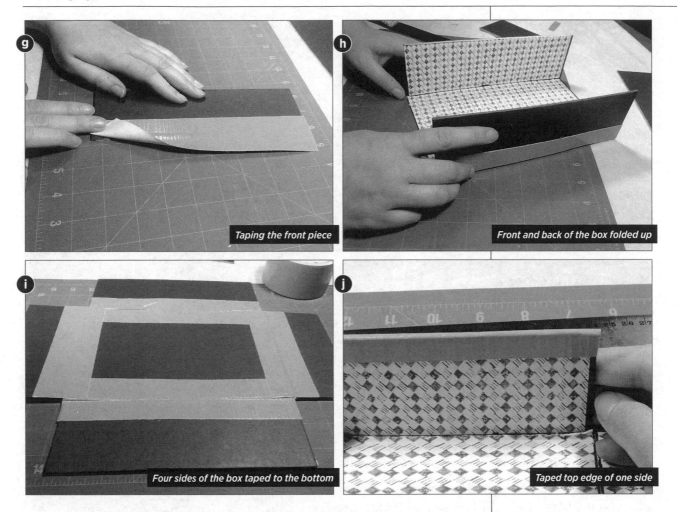

Taping the front piece

Front and back of the box folded up

Four sides of the box taped to the bottom

Taped top edge of one side

Holding the tape folded back out of the way, line up the edge against the bottom piece of the box. The tape will stretch a bit, so you can lay the pieces flat on the table, edge to edge, and press the tape into place. If you don't press the tape down all the way, you can adjust it a bit if you place it incorrectly the first time. After the tape is in place, you want to be able to fold the front piece up so that it rests on the very edge of the bottom piece of the box **[h]**. This isn't the most important detail, but it creates a cleaner finish. Don't stress out if it doesn't fit exactly—your box will still look fabulous.

Repeat the same steps to tape the back and two sides **[i]**.

3 Assembling the Box—Finishing the Edges

After you've taped all four sides of the box to the bottom, finish the exposed top edges of the front and sides with tape. Measure a piece of tape the length of the front piece. Place the tape along the outside edge, leaving some of the width of the tape overhanging the edge. Avoiding wrinkles, carefully fold the tape over the edge. Repeat for both side pieces **[j]**.

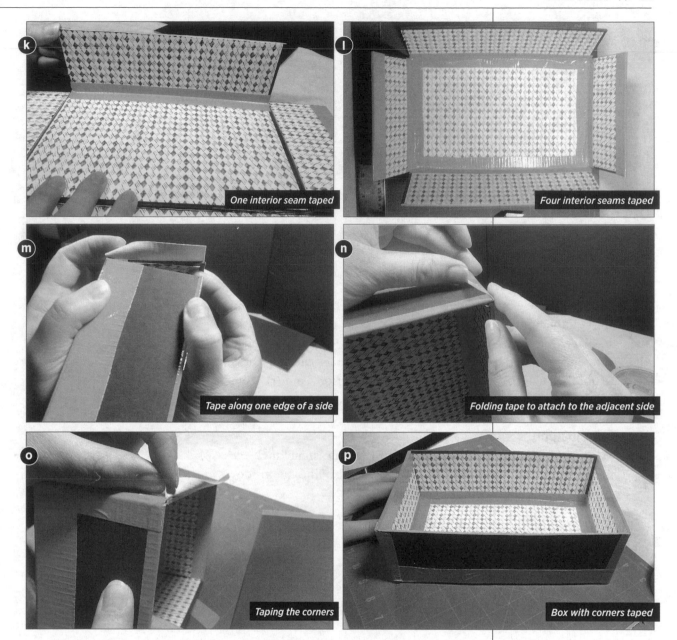

One interior seam taped

Four interior seams taped

Tape along one edge of a side

Folding tape to attach to the adjacent side

Taping the corners

Box with corners taped

4 **Assembling the Box—Taping the Inside**

To make the box more stable, you can tape the inside seams. Measure the tape to the length of a side and, while holding the side vertical, carefully place the tape along the seam **[k]**. This tape will hold the side up. Repeat the process for the remaining three sides **[l]**. It may get a little trickier as you go depending on the size of your box.

5 **Assembling the Box—Taping the Corners**

To tape the corners, measure the tape to fit the height of the box and place it along one edge of a side piece **[m]**. Fold the tape over to attach the two sides, carefully smoothing it down over the seam **[n]**. Tape all of the corners **[o, p]**. For added stability, you can tape the interior seams of the corners as well, but it's not absolutely necessary.

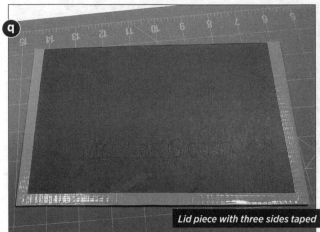

Lid piece with three sides taped

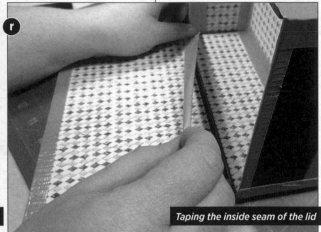

Taping the inside seam of the lid

6 Assembling the Box—Finishing the Lid

Tape the three exposed edges of the lid **[q]**. Then lay the lid flat on the table and stand the box up on its back to line it up with the lid piece. Measure a length of tape and place it along the outside edge of the lid. Attach the lid to the outside of the back piece of the box. Measure another length of tape to fit along the interior seam **[r]**. Your box is finished.

7 Embellishing

If you want, glitz up your box with paint, glitter, stenciling, stamping, or even beads or ribbon. You can also line the inside of the box with felt or colored paper.

quick-fire version

To simplify this project, you can precut the box pieces for each teen. Precutting also allows younger teens to do this project. Make sure to choose a wide variety of books of different colors, subjects, and cover designs, keeping in mind the group you're working with. Taping the books can go very quickly. Embellish as desired.

adaptations

While the need for patience and a steady hand may make this an unlikely choice for younger kids, adult crafters and seniors will really enjoy it. The finished boxes can be useful in a variety of ways (gift boxes, office organizers, stationery boxes, catchalls, recipe boxes, etc.), and providing some funny or nostalgic titles can inspire a lot of creativity.

polymer clay creatures

Difficulty:
Hard

Time:
Session 1—60 minutes (not including baking); Session 2—60 minutes

Supervision:
Medium

Group Size:
4–6 teens per librarian

Mess Factor:
Medium–high

mAKING THESE CLAY CHARACTERS CAN BE so much fun it's hard to stop at just one. Besides the nearly limitless options in putting them together, when the critters are done, you and your group can use them to make stop-motion videos, game pieces, comic strips, or other storytelling devices. Or they can just hang out on the shelves and look cool.

While leading a double session can be tricky, with the right planning, this project can be perfect for some of your teen campaigns. Work them into your Teen Tech Week and have teens use the finished characters to make a video about using the library. Or plan the project as part of your summer groups and tailor the designs to fit a theme. The end result can really be worth the extra effort.

Session 1

SUPPLIES AND TOOLS

- access to an oven (post project)
- cookie/baking sheets
- marker
- parchment paper
- short lengths of the same wire you plan to use for assembly (to poke the holes prior to baking)*
- small plastic cups or jars or short lengths of PVC pipe to use as rolling pins*
- toothpicks and plastic forks, spoons, and knives to use as modeling tools*
- wire cutters
- zip-close plastic sandwich bags*

MATERIALS

- Sculpey or other polymer modeling clay (assorted colors)

One for each participant

Session 2

SUPPLIES AND TOOLS

- drying trays or parchment paper
- needle-nose pliers*
- quick-drying glue
- wire cutters*

MATERIALS

- baked pieces from the previous session
- wire

One for every two participants

session 1: prep work

Getting the Project Ready

Read through the whole project and make copies of the directions to give to teens at the session. If possible, make a sample (or have one made) to display.

Figure out a plan for baking the clay pieces. If your library has access to an oven you might be able to get these sessions done back to back. If not, you will need to take the pieces home (or to an available kitchen) to bake.

One of the most critical steps in the first session is to make the holes that teens will use to assemble the creatures in session 2. These holes must be made before baking. The clay bakes too hard to make the holes after baking, and by that point it's usually too late to make a replacement part. Use wire cutters to cut short pieces for each participant from the wire that you have purchased for the second session.

Floral wire is usually a little cheaper in craft stores than jewelry wire. It also comes in a variety of anodized colors and in several weights or gauges. We recommend having both a thick wire and a thin wire available for teens to use. Thicker wire works better for attaching heads, hands, and feet, while thinner wire works well for ears, antennae, and other small appendages. When buying colored wire, it is very important that you get anodized wire, not wrapped wire [a].

As your teens finish their creature parts, have them put the pieces directly on the parchment paper on the cookie sheets, circle them, and

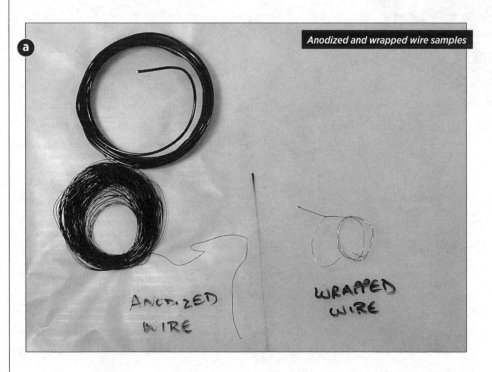

Anodized and wrapped wire samples

write their names in marker on the parchment nearby. This will make things much easier going into session 2. Another option is to use a digital camera to take photos of the prebaked pieces. If you're very conscientious, do both.

Getting the Room Ready

Cover the worktable. If you have carpet to protect, put some plastic down. Set wastebaskets around the table for easy cleanup. Display your samples. For each participant, put out a jar or piece of pipe for rolling, a selection of modeling tools, the short lengths of wire, and a sandwich bag. Centrally locate the clay on the worktable where everyone can get to the colors they need. Line the cookie sheets with the parchment paper and set them aside.

Before getting started, show the group your sample and explain the basics of the project. You may want to go over the instructions with the group, or give the teens a few minutes to read through the directions on their own and then answer any questions they may have.

directions

Read all of the instructions first!

1 Modeling a Creature

Work the clay to soften it while you consider what kind of creature to make: robot, alien, swamp thing? These creatures can look like anything—it is entirely up to you. (Steer clear of giants, though. They take a long time to bake and use a large amount of clay.) Simple shapes are quick and easy to make with the clay. Think in terms of what body parts you will need—head, hands, feet, body, tail, antennae, eyes, and so on [b]. Use your imagination! Modeling tools can help you add details or make shapes.

If you want, press together pieces of different colors. For example, add clay details onto the body to look like clothing, or add eyes to your creature's face [c]. Adding a piece like this usually requires just a bit of pressure and smoothing the edges together.

As you work, think about how you want to put the creature together and where to attach

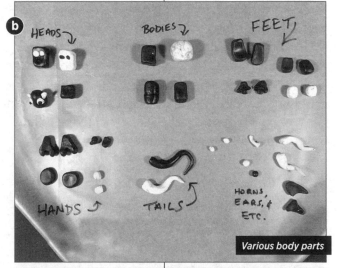

Various body parts

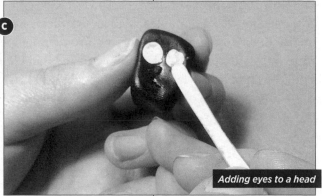

Adding eyes to a head

the wires. Plan how to attach the appendages to the body and how to position the limbs. Make sure your creature will be able to stand on its feet. This means making them big enough to support the figure, but also flat enough on the bottom not to fall over **[d]**.

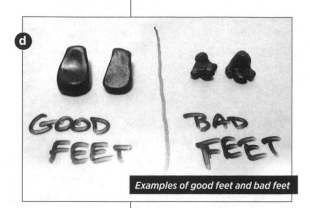

Examples of good feet and bad feet

2 Making the Wire Holes

After you have made all of your pieces, lay them out in the positions they will be in when assembled **[e]**. With a piece of wire, make the holes that you will use in the next session to put the creature together. Start with the head and work down **[f]**. The depth of the holes will depend on how big the piece is and on how many holes are going to be needed in that piece. Try for about ⅛–¼ inch deep. If your piece falls apart as you're making your holes, you'll need to remake that piece in a slightly larger size.

Clay pieces laid out in order

3 Preparing for Baking

Lay your pieces on the cookie sheet lined with parchment paper. You can keep them in the shape of the creature, but it's not necessary. Write your name on the parchment and draw a circle around your name and pieces so everyone knows which creature is yours **[g]**.

As you are cleaning up, put the pieces of wire you used to poke your holes in a sandwich bag and put your name on it so you'll know what type of wire you'll need for assembly.

Poking wire hole in a head

session 2: prep work

Getting the Project Ready

After session 1, bake the teens' pieces. Follow the instructions on the clay's packaging for oven temperature and time. After the pieces have baked and cooled, put them into sandwich bags and label the bags with the teens' names. You can even use the bags that contain the teens' wire snippets.

Getting the Room Ready

Once again cover the tables and set out wastebaskets. As wire gets clipped small pieces may scatter, so have

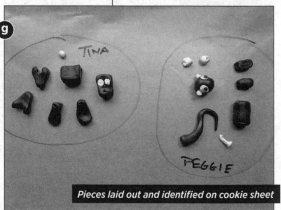

Pieces laid out and identified on cookie sheet

teens pick up scraps from the floor as they go. Put out the prebaked pieces. Set wire, tools, and glue in the center of the worktable.

Before getting started, review the assembly instructions with the teens and answer any questions they may have.

directions

Read all of the instructions first!

1 Laying Out and Double Checking the Pieces

Lay out your clay pieces as they will be put together [h]. As you do, double check to make sure you have all of the holes you need in the proper places. If you're missing a hole, you may need to rethink your creature's design.

2 Assembling the Pieces— Hands, Feet, and Other Appendages

Clip your wire into short lengths for your creature's arms and legs and whatever other appendages you've made [i]. The wires don't need to be cut to the final length yet; just be sure that they are a little longer than you need and you'll be able to trim them down later.

Start by testing the wire in the holes for the appendages. It should fit into the holes snugly. Use pliers to push the wire into the hole as far as it will go [j]. Don't do this with your hands because the wire can be very sharp.

After making sure the wire fits into the hole, take it out, put a small bit of glue on the tip of the wire, and push it back into the hole [k]. Put the piece aside to dry and repeat this process with the rest of the creature's appendages.

3 Assembling the Pieces—the Body

After you have glued the wires into place on your creature's appendages, start attaching the parts to the main body of your creature [l]. As you test the fit of the wire to the holes, also decide how long your creature's arms and legs (tail,

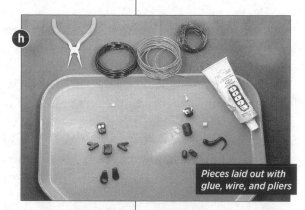
Pieces laid out with glue, wire, and pliers

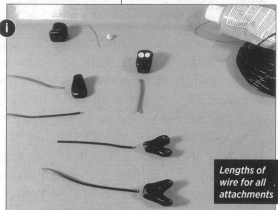
Lengths of wire for all attachments

Pushing wire into a baked clay piece with pliers

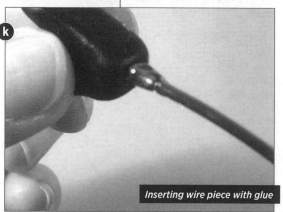
Inserting wire piece with glue

tentacles—whatever) should be. The length depends largely on design, but keep in mind that the creature should be able to stand on its own.

After you trim the wires to the lengths you want and everything is even, add the dab of glue to the ends of the wire and glue the pieces into place [m]. Set your creature aside to dry while you pick up your stray wire clippings and tidy your area and the floor around you.

4 Posing

After your creature is dry enough to handle, you can pose the limbs. This is a delicate process, so be careful. Use the needle-nose pliers to gently bend the wires of the arms and legs [n]. Bend and shape the limbs until they look good. Try to keep the pressure on the wire itself and don't pull or press too hard on the recently glued joint.

Test the stance of the legs. You may need to shift and bend the wires of the legs a few times to get your creature to stand. If your creature has a tail, it can help stabilize the stance. Shift the other appendages to adjust balance, as needed.

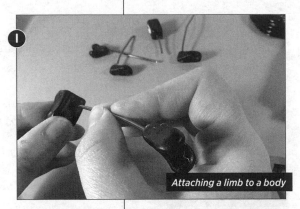
Attaching a limb to a body

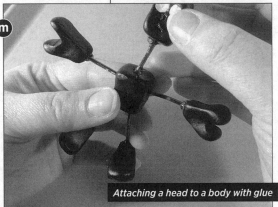
Attaching a head to a body with glue

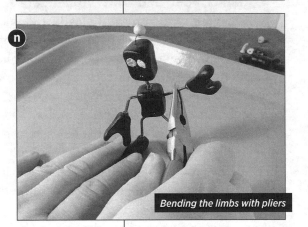
Bending the limbs with pliers

quick-fire version

Here are two variations that will cut time by limiting the project to a single session.

- **Option 1**—Have the teens make a single solid piece with the clay that won't require assembly later. This cuts down on poseability, but it's still fun to play with clay. You will still need a plan for baking the clay.

- **Option 2**—Mold, poke holes in, and bake the component pieces yourself and let the teens put the creatures together. Because this option makes the assembly more of an à la carte process, you'll need to make a lot of different options to ensure that it will still be an entertaining project for teens. Shapes can be simple (spheres, cubes, cylinders, etc.), but you will need to make executive decisions about where the holes go. Be sure to add the holes before baking.

adaptations

This project would make a fun parent-child or mentor-mentee project with few or no changes.

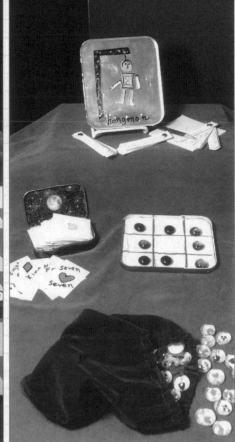

make your own games

Difficulty:
Medium

Time:
60–90 minutes

Supervision:
Heavy

Group Size:
4–6 teens per
librarian

Mess Factor:
Medium

GAMES IN THE LIBRARY CAN BE TONS OF FUN, AND MAKING your own versions stems out of that naturally. While the games we've listed below are familiar standbys, we learned so much about them (and games in general) just by looking at them in a new way. This project can create an opportunity for discussion about how games came to be, where they come from, and how they develop. And once teens learn how to make these basic games, they can branch out into making games of their own.

We've put this project at the end as an example of how the techniques we used for previous projects can be applied to something new. In a library setting this would be a fun project to do to call attention to your gaming collection or if you're planning an event for National Gaming Day. If you use these techniques to have teens make their own game, you can work it into almost any teen program you have going on, from reading groups to anime clubs. If you have a larger group of teens, you can have them break into teams and compete to make the best game.

SUPPLIES AND TOOLS

- box cutter or craft knife
- carbon or transfer paper
- craft glue
- deck of playing cards (for reference)
- decoupage medium
- game instructions (available on the Internet)
- paint pens
- paintbrushes
- pencils and pens
- permanent markers
- rulers
- scissors
- stamps and ink pads

MATERIALS

- assorted embellishments (stickers, glitter, clip art, etc.)
- assorted hardware (nuts, bolts, washers, etc.)
- assorted small tins or boxes
- button magnets
- card stock
- cardboard
- cork tiles
- craft marbles (some clear and colorless and some sets of different colors)
- craft paint and craft sticks
- dice salvaged from old games or purchased
- duct tape (assorted colors and patterns)
- fabric scrap (canvas, denim, felt; durable, heavy-weight fabrics work best)
- magnet sheet (or recycle old flat magnet calendars, ads, etc.)
- objects for game tokens (pushpins, bottle caps, buttons, small mosaic tiles, beads, recycled game tokens, etc.)
- packing tape
- paper scrap
- scrapbook paper
- small notepads and pencils
- wooden trays or box lids

prep work

Getting the Project Ready

Read through the whole project and make copies of the directions to give to teens at the session. If possible, make a sample (or have one made) to display. If you plan to use wooden craft sticks for game tokens, cut them down to game-piece size to save a bit of time during the session. You can also cut the card stock into small playing-card sizes and the scrapbook paper into strips to be used for game boards. For flat magnet pieces you can use old advertising magnets or magnet calendars: cover the tops with duct tape and trim off the excess tape **[a]**.

Getting the Room Ready

Cover the worktable. Set wastebaskets around the table for easy cleanup. Display your sample game. Place the scissors, box cutter, rulers, pencils, pens, and markers in the center of the worktable. Arrange the materials on a side table, sorted by type (for instance, put the board-making materials together and the token-making materials together, and so on).

Before getting started, show the group your sample and explain the basics of the project. You may want to go over the instructions with the group, or give the teens a few minutes to read through the directions on their own and then answer any questions they may have.

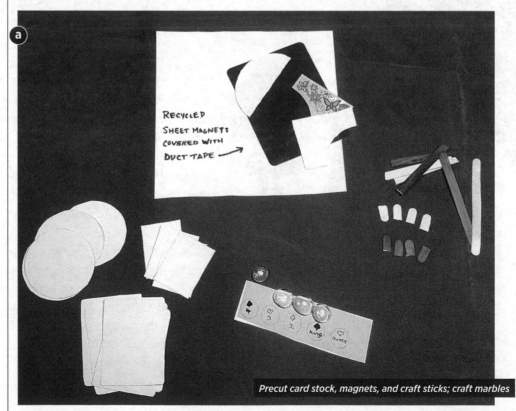

Precut card stock, magnets, and craft sticks; craft marbles

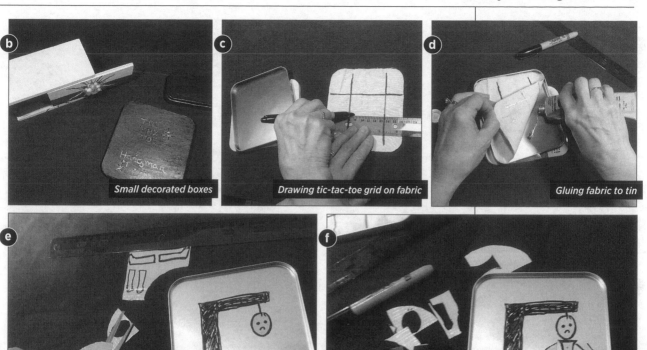

Small decorated boxes

Drawing tic-tac-toe grid on fabric

Gluing fabric to tin

Cutting body parts out of magnet

Sample hanged man

directions

Read all of the instructions first!

Making nonboard games

TIC TAC TOE OR HANGMAN GAME TIN
(VERY SIMPLE)

These two simple games are easy to complete and can fit into one small tin.

Begin by painting the outside of the tin and embellishing it any way you want (see the Decorated Containers project) **[b]**.

For tic-tac-toe, choose six craft marbles in each of two different colors for the tokens. Cut a piece of sturdy fabric for the game board; draw the game grid onto fabric with permanent markers **[c]** and glue it to the inside bottom of the tin **[d]**.

The hangman game is just as easy to make. Use a permanent marker to draw the hangman board on the inside of the tin's lid. Cut a magnet into body part shapes (head, arms, legs, body) **[e, f]**. Add a small notepad and pencil for spelling out the words.

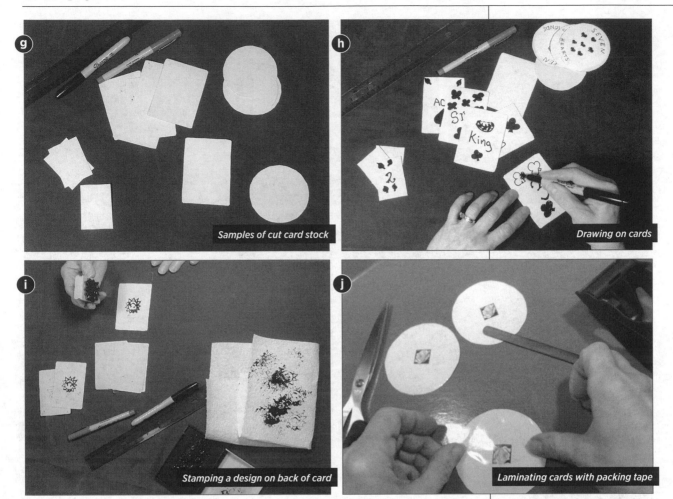

g — Samples of cut card stock

h — Drawing on cards

i — Stamping a design on back of card

j — Laminating cards with packing tape

PLAYING CARDS (SIMPLE)

Cut 54 pieces of card stock to playing-card size; you can make regular-sized cards or mini cards, or even circles, squares, or another shape, as long as all 54 cards are the same **[g]**.

If you want, paint and decorate a tin to keep the cards in (see the Decorated Containers project). A tin is optional but nice for keeping the cards together.

Draw the card suits (hearts, diamonds, clubs, and spades) on the card stock, using the regular deck of cards for reference if you need to **[h]**. Each suit needs an ace, a king, a queen, a jack, number cards from two to ten, and two jokers. Your jokers can be as simple or as elaborate as you want.

The backs of all 54 cards need to be decorated exactly the same. We used a stamp for our sample **[i]**. You can use stickers or clip art or scrap-book paper cut into identical pieces.

After you decorate the cards, laminate them with packing tape to make them more durable and easier to use **[j]**.

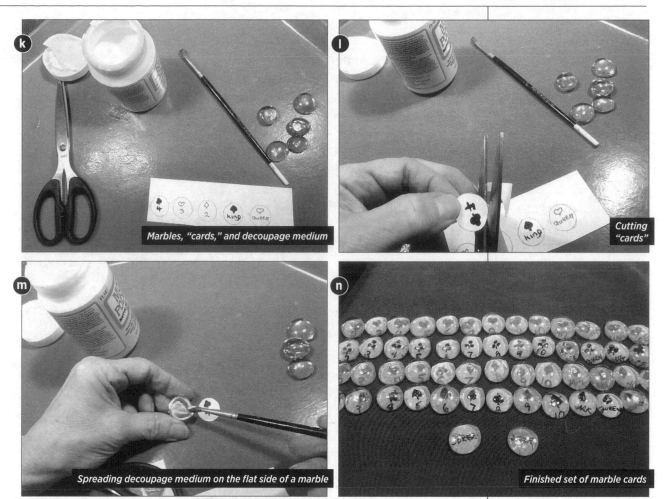

Marbles, "cards," and decoupage medium

Cutting "cards"

Spreading decoupage medium on the flat side of a marble

Finished set of marble cards

CRAFT MARBLE PLAYING CARDS (SIMPLE)

For a really nontraditional take on playing cards, you can make a "deck" out of craft marbles. You would make this almost exactly like you would marble magnets (see the first *Teen Craft Projects* book for instructions on making marble magnets).

First draw out mini symbols for your "cards." Given the small space, you'll need to abbreviate and be more stylistic about your representations. On ours we opted to draw the suit symbol (heart, club, diamond, or spade) and a number (2–10) or letter (for the face cards and the aces: A = ace, K = king, Q = queen, J = jack) **[k]**.

Once you have your mini symbols drawn, cut them down to fit your 54 marbles **[l]**. Decoupage the pictures to the flat side of the marbles and let them dry **[m]**.

We put our card marbles in a nice drawstring bag that we happened to have, but you could store them in a decorated tin or make your own bag.

Making board games

Most board games require boards and tokens, so they are a little more complex but still fun to create. Materials also offer a lot of design possibilities. For instance, a fabric board is more portable and more durable than cardboard, and a corkboard allows for pushpin pieces. Just be sure to make the board first and then the pieces, or else you may have a board that's too small or tokens that don't fit on the board.

CHECKERS (SIMPLE)

Making the Board

Use the template on page 82 to make a grid with 64 squares of two alternating colors **[o]**. You can make the board out of almost anything:

- thin cardboard covered with duct tape
- a box lid or wooden tray decoupaged with scrapbook paper
- a box lid, wooden tray, or cork or wooden tile with a grid painted on
- canvas or denim with a fabric-paint grid
- plain checked fabric (a *really* easy shortcut)
- laminated paper strips woven into a mat (like the woven magazine baskets in the first *Teen Craft Projects*)

Making the Checkers

Checkers are basically just round, stackable disks. You need 24 total—12 each in two different colors. You have many options for making and decorating the checkers. Bottle caps, buttons, and washers or bolts all work well, but keep in mind that all the pieces need to be the same size and shape **[p]**.

Once you have your checkers picked out, you can decorate them. You can use paint (although it may not work with some types of plastics), stickers, or paper scrap decoupage, or you can do a free-form design with permanent markers. It's a small space so it's best not to get too complicated.

Sample boards

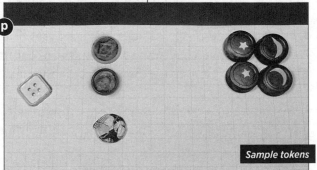

Sample tokens

CHESS (SIMPLE TO MEDIUM)

Making the Board

Chess uses the same board as checkers, so use the directions on page 24. Remember, though, that your chess pieces need to fit on the board, so keep the size of your pieces in mind when planning your board.

Making the Pieces

Chess needs 32 pieces, 16 of each color. You don't need to stick to black and white. You could do red vs. blue, pink vs. purple, or even stripes vs. polka dots. However, you must have these pieces for each side: one king, one queen, two rooks, two knights, two bishops, and eight pawns. There is no set rule about what the pieces need to look like, but follow these general suggestions to make playing the game easier:

- Make pawns all the same height, and shorter than the other pieces.
- Make sure it's easy to differentiate the two opposing sides (for example, all the pieces on the red side should have red on them).
- Try to make the two rooks and the two bishops on the same side look similar.
- If you're making three-dimensional pieces, the king and the queen should be the tallest pieces.

Here are a few suggestions for creating your pieces:

Hardware. For something different, try hardware **[q]**. Use nuts, bolts, washers, and other fun bits of hardware to build pieces. Use a bolt as the base. Then screw on nuts and washers. Not every nut or washer needs to be screwed all the way down the bolt. After you

Hardware chess pieces

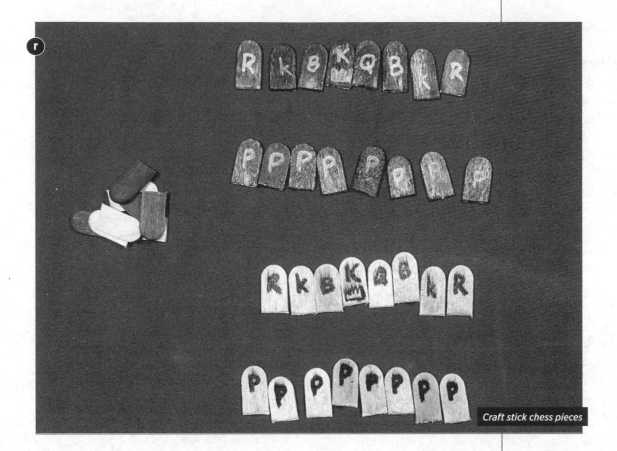

Craft stick chess pieces

complete all of your pieces, you can paint some or all of them as needed to differentiate sides. Keep in mind that these pieces can end up being quite heavy.

Polymer Clay. Using the techniques in the Polymer Clay Creatures project, you can make your pieces as wild as you want (as long as they stand up and take up only one square apiece). Using clay will take more than one session, however, because the pieces have to be baked.

Flat Tokens. You can make a very minimalist chess set by using flat pieces. Try using pieces of wooden craft sticks **[r]**, craft marbles, small mosaic tiles, buttons, bottle caps, or even cardboard. After you've cut your pieces to size, make the two sides distinct. You can simply write what the piece is with marker or pen or use stickers or stamps to mark them (for example, little crowns for the kings, swords for the pawns, etc.). Once you've finished decorating, you should coat the pieces to protect the art. Laminate cardboard pieces with packing tape or coat wooden pieces with decoupage.

Other Ideas for Pieces. If you don't have hardware on hand, you can use beads instead. Or you can glue buttons into stacks. You can even repurpose game tokens from other games.

PARCHEESI (MEDIUM)

Making the Board

On the surface a Parcheesi board looks complicated, but it's mostly lines and some simple shapes. You divide the main cross of the board into 72 spaces with a "home" space in the middle and four starting points in the corners of the board. We've included a basic template on page 83, but if you have time and a straightedge you can make your own from scratch.

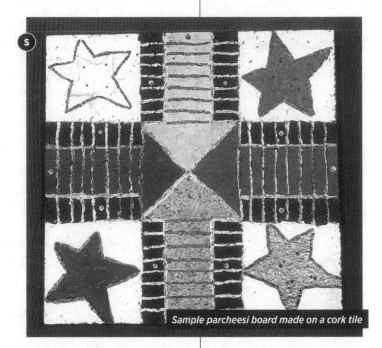

Sample parcheesi board made on a cork tile

The most straightforward way to make this board is to paint or draw it on a surface. Cloth works very well (a sturdy denim or canvas), or use the lid of a good-sized cookie tin. For something different you can use a cork tile with pushpins for game pieces **[s]**.

If you need to, use a photocopier to enlarge the board template. Then use carbon or transfer paper to trace it onto the fabric or other board material. Go over the lines with paint pen or permanent marker. Then color the board. Use paint or decoupage in whatever colors or patterns you'd like to create the four starting spaces: for example, green, blue, red, and yellow; or black, white, red, and gray; or stripes, plaid, polka-dot, and paisley.

Making the Pieces

For game play you will need four tokens in each of four different colors to match the four starting spots. The tokens don't need to be complicated. You can use craft marbles, beads, buttons, or any small pieces that are uniform in size and shape. You can decorate the pieces, if you'd like, but we recommend keeping it simple. Just a dab of paint or glitter here and there.

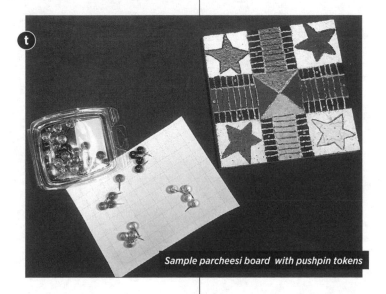

Sample parcheesi board with pushpin tokens

As we said above, if you used cork for your board, you can use pushpins for your pieces **[t]**. If you used a metal tin for your board, you can make craft marbles into magnets for your tokens, or decorate button magnets.

After your game board and pieces are finished, you'll need two six-sided dice to play.

quick-fire version

To simplify this project we recommend choosing one game and limiting the materials. For example, have everyone make checkers with a fabric board and bottle-cap tokens.

adaptations

This project would be fun for groups. As a family, parents and children can make a whole set of games. Making larger versions of the simpler games can be fun for younger kids or developmentally disabled patrons. Be sure to provide materials that are easier to use for these groups.

templates

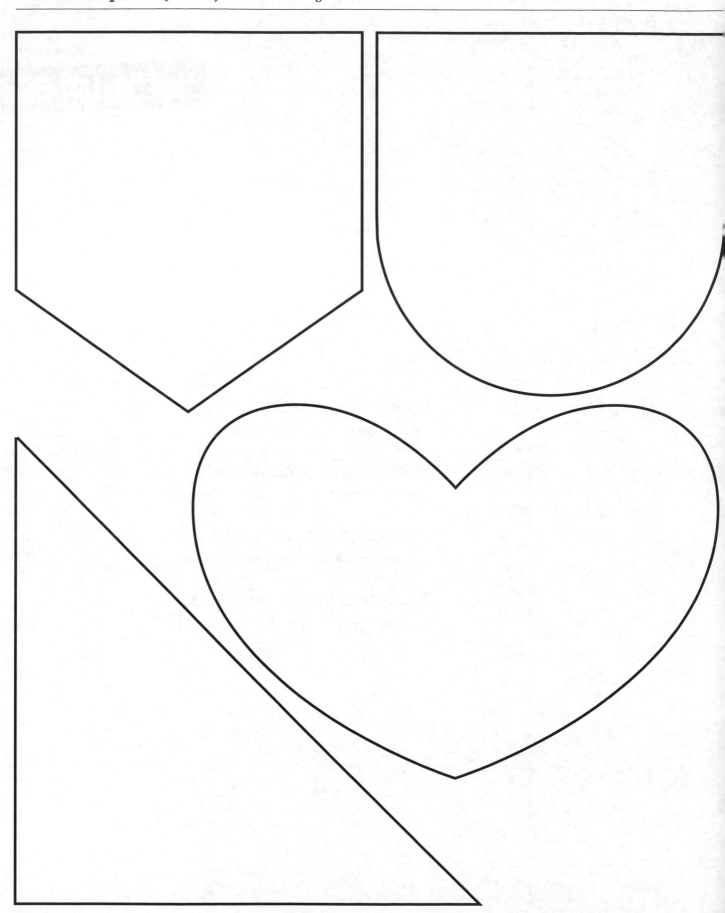

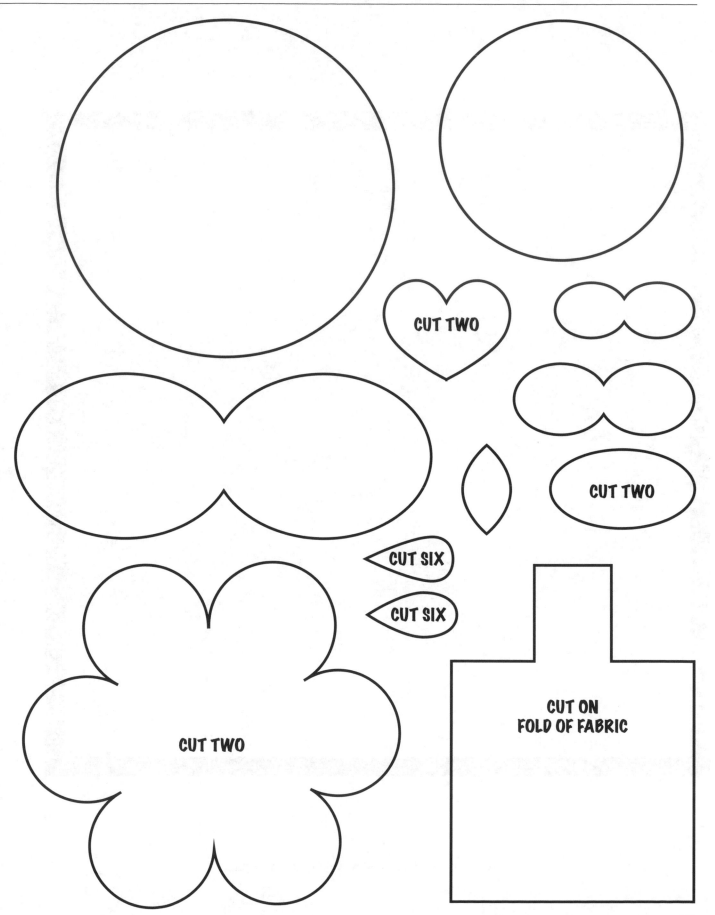

CUT TWO

CUT TWO

CUT SIX

CUT SIX

CUT TWO

CUT ON
FOLD OF FABRIC

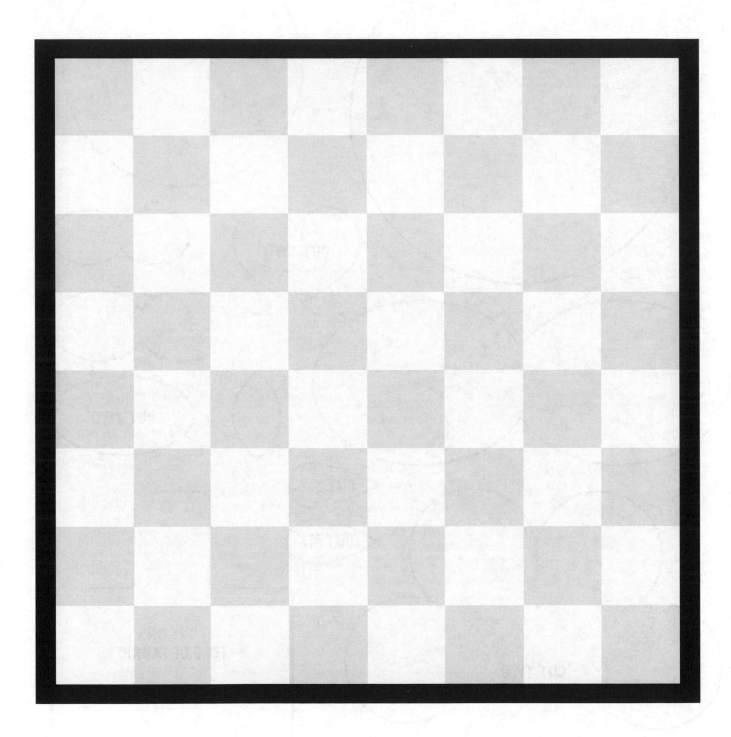

Enlarge to desired size (150% will fit on 11 x 17 paper)

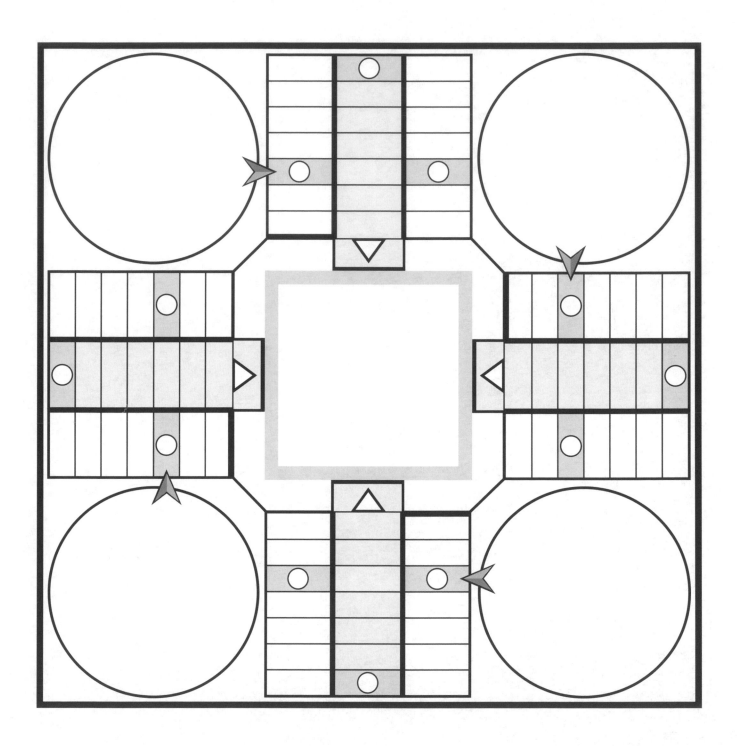

Enlarge to desired size (150% will fit on 11 x 17 paper)

supplies, tools, and project materials

Supplies and Tools List

- awl
- box cutter or craft knife
- brick, flat stone, or block of wood (for pushing needles through cardboard)
- carbon or transfer paper
- cardboard
    - heavy, to use as cutting mats
    - lightweight, for making templates
- containers (small; for sorting materials)
- cookie/baking sheets
- crayons
- cups, jars, or short lengths of PVC pipe (for rolling clay)
- cutting mats or heavy cardboard
- decoupage medium
- drill (small) or Dremel tool
- drop cloths or reusable plastic tablecloths
- egg cartons (Styrofoam)
- envelopes (various sizes; for making templates)
- game instructions (for various games; find them on the Internet)
- glue
    - craft glue
    - glue sticks (plain and glitter)
    - hot glue
    - quick-drying glue
- grommet setter
- hammer

- hole punch (heavy-duty)
- ink pads
- iron, ironing board (or towel), and pressing cloth
- markers
  - fabric
  - permanent
  - regular
- oven (for baking clay)
- paint pens
- paintbrushes
- paper towels
- parchment paper
- pencils and pens
- plastic forks, spoons, and knives (for modeling clay)
- playing cards
- pliers
  - jewelry or needle-nose
  - regular
- poster board or lightweight cardboard
- rubber stamps
- rulers
  - metal
  - large, for use as straightedge
  - regular
- sandwich bags (plastic zip-close type)
- scissors
  - pinking shears
  - regular
  - scrapbooking
- scrapbook templates
- screwdriver, flathead
- sewing needles
  - large, for sewing through cardboard
  - large-eyed, for embroidery floss
  - medium, for regular sewing
- shoe boxes
- sponges (small; for applying paint)
- staple gun
- staplers
- stencils and stencil brushes
- tape, masking

- thimbles (metal)
- toothpicks
- trays (plastic or Styrofoam)
- wet wipes
- wire cutters

Materials List
- address labels (blank)
- barrette blanks
- batting
- binder clips
- books, hardcover (pulled from circulation)
- box lids
- brads (plain brass or fancier scrapbooking brads)
- buckles
- card stock
- cardboard (various thicknesses and textures)
- CD spools
- CDs, recycled
- containers, tins, and boxes (assorted sizes and styles)
- cork tiles
- craft foam sheets (plain and glitter)
- craft marbles (clear colorless and colored)
- craft sticks (wooden)
- D rings
- dice (salvaged from old games or purchased)
- dowels
- embellishments (including badges; beads; buckles; buttons; chain scraps; charms; clip art; craft foam shapes; game tokens; glitter; hardware; jewelry pieces; jewels; key chains; keys; lace; leather scraps from belts, purse straps, shoes, etc.; miniatures; pins; ribbon; sequins; small toys; stickers; stones; yarn)
- embroidery floss
- fabric (including heavy cotton, denim, medium- to heavy-weight knit or flannel, upholstery fabric, felt)

- fabric scrap (including canvas, cotton, denim, felt, flannel, fleece, lace, leather, suede, voile; quilting squares; cuffs from shirts; waistbands and belt loops from jeans and pants)
- game tokens (beads, bottle caps, buttons, pushpins, recycled tokens from purchased games, small mosaic tiles)
- grommets
- hardware (nuts, bolts, washers, etc.)
- iron-on fusible web
- jewelry scraps (including bangles; chains; charms, pendants, and other pieces; hoop earrings in various shapes)
- jump rings
- key rings (assorted sizes)
- lacing materials (including cord, leather strap, ribbon, twine, yarn)
- magnets
  • button
  • sheet (purchased or recycled)
- mirrors (small; recycled from makeup compacts or purses, or purchased)
- nails (small)
- notepads and pencils (small)
- paint (including acrylic, craft, stencil, tempera, watercolor)
- paint, fabric (including glitter, puffy, regular)
- paper (including colored, scrapbook, white)
- paper clips
- paper scrap (old maps, magazines, weeded books, etc.)
- picture frames (large)
- picture hangers and wire
- pin backs, bar-style
- pipe cleaners
- poster board
- safety pins
- Sculpey or other polymer modeling clay

- snaps (sew-on)
- staples (regular and heavy-duty)
- tape
  • duct tape
  • gaffers tape
  • packing tape
- thread
- toggle closures
- trays (wooden; for making game boards)
- Velcro (self-stick squares or dots)
- vellum quotes
- wire
  • floral
  • jewelry

glossary

Techniques

We use several techniques repeatedly in projects throughout the book. Although they are described in the project instructions, here are more distinct definitions or details on how to do them.

BURNISH. To rub with a tool that is specially made for smoothing and polishing. We use this technique in laminating some of our paper projects.

DECOUPAGE. To decorate with cutouts of paper, fabric, or other flat material over which polyurethane is applied. This is a sure-fire technique that anyone can do.

Hand Sewing

BLANKET STITCH. A blanket stitch is a variation on a whipstitch. You start with a whip **[a]**, then bring your needle through your thread loop **[b]** and pull tightly **[c]**. Your stitches can be farther apart. Use this stitch for decorative outside seams. It also works well for topstitching.

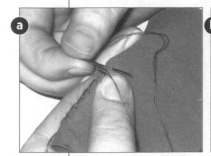

Blanket stitch

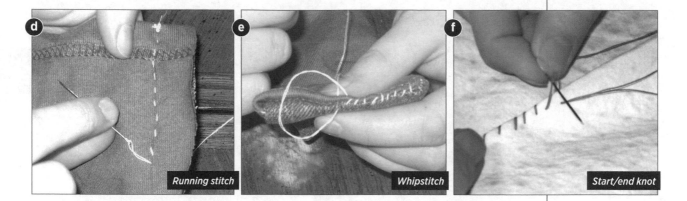

Running stitch — *Whipstitch* — *Start/end knot*

RUNNING STITCH. A running stitch is a basic in-and-out stitch **[d]**. It's mostly used for inside seams that will not be seen once the fabric is turned inside out, so precise alignment is not critical.

WHIPSTITCH. A whipstitch is a basic stitch that goes over the edge of the seam with the needle always coming up through the fabric in the same direction **[e]**. It is mostly used for outside seams or decorative touches.

START/END KNOT. Pull the thread through the fabric, leaving a tail. Sew another stitch, this time bringing your needle through the thread loop. Pull tightly, holding the tail as you do. This creates a knot that will anchor your seam **[f]**.

Tools and Materials

ADHESIVES. Hot-glue guns and glue sticks can be used for these projects. However, hot glue, though a quick solution, is not always permanent. Sometimes other glues are a better and more permanent choice. It's also a good idea to have options on hand if you can. When choosing fabric glue, read the label and make sure it is permanent and washable. Bead/jewelry glue is a quick-set glue and adheres to many surfaces, but it can be messy so make sure to cover the work area. Participants may want to wear disposable plastic gloves.

BEADING NEEDLE. A beading needle is a flexible piece of thin wire with a sharp point and a large eye that will fit through most beads. They are available at most craft supply stores in the beading section.

BURNISHING TOOL. A burnishing tool is a slim, hard plastic stick with a slightly wider curved head. You can improvise a burnishing tool by using a craft stick. In a pinch, your fingernail will work.

CARDBOARD. Several of the projects here call for cardboard in various weights. It's always good to have a supply on hand. Heavier weights from boxes are always useful. If you run across cardboard with interesting textures like egg-carton or corrugated, be sure to add it to your stash.

EMBELLISHMENTS. Embellishments are easily one of the most important materials to have in good supply. Looked at properly, anything can be used as an embellishment. Here are just a few examples of things you should hoard:

- beads
- computer or other electronic circuit boards
- costume jewelry
- game or puzzle pieces (collect them from games that are already missing pieces)
- key chains
- recycled ribbons, yarn, twine (these are easy to find during the holidays)
- sequins
- small mirrors (you can recycle the mirrors from makeup cases and purses)
- small toys
- watches and clocks

FABRIC SCRAP. You can find fabric scrap all around—your own closet, garage sales, resale shops, and donations. Some things to look for:

- clothing (keep an eye out for leather and suede especially; recycling a leather skirt from a thrift shop is much cheaper than buying leather from a fabric shop)
- curtains
- fabric remnants
- neckties
- quilting squares
- recycled denims (jeans, shirts, skirts, etc.; denim is one of the easiest fabrics to get and is also very easy to work with)
- table or bed linens

GROMMET PLIERS AND GROMMETS. Grommet pliers are special pliers that you can use to punch holes and install grommets. They are available at most sewing, craft, or art supply stores. The instructions on how to use them are on the packaging, so be sure to keep the package or photocopy the instructions to keep with the pliers. Grommets come in different colors and sizes and should be available in the same aisle.

HAND SEWING SUPPLIES. For any sewing project you should have some basic hand sewing supplies for each participant. The following are recommended:

- embroidery floss (assorted colors)
- measuring tape
- needle threaders
- needles (assorted)
- pincushions
- safety pins
- seam rippers
- straight pins
- tailor's chalk or something to mark fabric with
- thimbles
- threads (black and white and several basic colors)

PACKING TAPE. We use packing tape as an easy seam closer and as a laminating material. We cannot stress enough how important it is to use good-quality tape in the right width. If you're going to splurge on anything, do it on this item. You want a thicker gauge tape about 2½ to 3 inches wide. Stay away from the cheap, thin packing tape; it will only stress you out. Be sure to have a good tape dispenser on hand as well.

PAPER SCRAP. This is another resource with almost endless uses. Decoupage anything and everything, and use pictures for jewelry, magnets, or paper baskets. Some ideas to get you started:

- book jackets
- books (discarded or damaged travel books, art books, graphic novels, children's books— especially those with bold, artsy pictures)
- calendars
- catalogs
- comics
- greeting cards or postcards (especially those with a vintage or graphic look)
- magazines
- maps
- posters

TABLE COVERING. Although you can use newspaper in a pinch, it's not particularly practical because it can get messy as you work. We recommend using cheap plastic tablecloths from the dollar store or recycling heavy-duty vinyl tablecloths you or your patrons may have on hand.

TRAYS (STYROFOAM OR PLASTIC). Trays are very helpful for keeping the teens organized as they work. Trays make cleanup a little easier as well. You can use Styrofoam trays (recycled from a cafeteria or purchased at a restaurant supply store); plastic cafeteria trays (you may find these at schools, hospital tag sales, garage sales, or discount stores); or clean, recycled Styrofoam food trays (you can save these from your own supply and/or ask for donations).

resources

Books

Blakeney, Faith, Justina Blakeney, Anka Livakovic, and Ellen Schultz. *99 Ways to Cut, Sew, Trim, and Tie Your T-shirt into Something Special.* Potter Craft, 2006.

The Complete Photo Guide to Sewing. Singer Sewing Reference Library. Creative Publishing, 1999.

Easy Beading. Better Homes and Gardens, 2004.

Maresh, Janice Saunders. *Sewing for Dummies.* For Dummies, 2004.

Nicolay, Megan. *Generation T: 108 Ways to Transform a T-shirt.* Workman, 2006.

Websites

Antimony & Lace (www.gothfashion.info)—Check the Projects tab for a list of clothing reconstruction projects that are fun for the gothic-ly inclined. Great for budding fashionistas.

Craftster (www.craftster.org)—A valuable resource for ideas with a great forum for showing off finished projects and sharing tutorials. This site also has regular contests and swaps. A great way to get into the cool crafting community, no matter what kinds of crafts you do.

Daydreaming on Paper (www.daydreamingonpaper.com)—A fabulous website on journaling with writing prompts and ideas on what to do with blank books.

DIY Network (www.DIYnetwork.com)—DIY and its sister station HGTV now have tons of crafter-friendly shows on the air. This site has projects for the crafty as well as more advanced projects.

Get Crafty (www.getcrafty.com)—More forums to share ideas, tutorials, and finished projects.

LiveJournal (www.livejournal.com)—LiveJournal is huge with tons of communities that change on almost a daily basis, but it's worthwhile to do a search under Interests for "crafts," "crafting," or "crafter" to find communities that allow for showing off projects and swapping ideas.

Stencil Revolution (www.stencilrevolution.com)—Great tutorials on how to make your own stencils with various techniques, tips on materials, and a place to show off projects.

You may also be interested in

THE HIPSTER LIBRARIAN'S GUIDE TO TEEN CRAFT PROJECTS

Tina Coleman and Peggie Llanes

The authors' focus on recycled no-cost and low-cost materials addresses most librarians' budget constraints. These craft sessions offer a unique way for teens to claim their identities and gain confidence—at the library!

ISBN: 978-0-8389-0971-3
104 pages / 8.5" x 11"

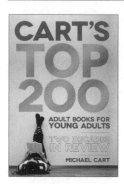

CART'S TOP 200 ADULT BOOKS FOR YOUNG ADULTS: Two Decades in Review

Michael Cart
ISBN: 978-0-8389-1105-1

INTELLECTUAL FREEDOM FOR TEENS: A Practical Guide for Young Adult & School Librarians

Kristin Fletcher-Spear and Kelly Tyler for YALSA
ISBN: 978-0-8389-1200-3

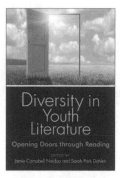

DIVERSITY IN YOUTH LITERATURE: Opening Doors through Reading

Jamie Campbell Naidoo and Sarah Park Dahlen
ISBN: 978-0-8389-1143-3

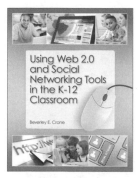

USING WEB 2.0 AND SOCIAL NETWORKING TOOLS IN THE K-12 CLASSROOM

Beverley E. Crane
ISBN: 978-1-55570-774-3

A YEAR OF PROGRAMS FOR TEENS 2

Amy J. Alessio and Kimberly A. Patton
ISBN: 978-0-8389-1051-1

EXPLORING ENVIRONMENTAL SCIENCE WITH CHILDREN AND TEENS

Eileen G. Harrington
ISBN: 978-0-8389-1198-3

Order today at alastore.ala.org or 866-746-7252!

ALA Store purchases fund advocacy, awareness, and accreditation programs for library professionals worldwide.